HIGH PEAK WALKS
by
Mark Richards

Commemorative plaque in Bowden Bridge Quarry car park
(WALK 14)

HIGH PEAK WALKS
by
Mark Richards

Front Cover: The Trinnacle - Ravenstones. Walk 2.
Back Cover: Bleaklow Groughs

ISBN 0 902363 43 1
© Mark Richards 1982
First published 1982
Reprinted 1983, 1985, 1987, 1989

Dedicated to Alison and Daniel

for their infectious love of life

Published by Cicerone Press,
Harmony Hall, Milnthorpe, Cumbria.

CONTENTS

FOREWORD

I first met Mark Richards several years ago when we were brought together by Roger Smith, the Editor of *The Great Outdoors*, for a day's walking in the Forest of Dean. His exquisite cartography and beautiful line drawings were well known to me and I had long admired his work so I was naturally very keen to meet him. Since that first walk together we have become firm friends, have collaborated on a number of books and I greatly enjoy visiting his family in their lovely Cotswold farmhouse.

Like so many gifted people he is modest almost to a fault. He is proud to describe himself as a pupil of Alfred Wainwright yet, as this guide proves, the erstwhile apprentice is now a master craftsman.

He not only maps and draws the countryside in remarkable detail but he also communicates his love of the British landscape and his understanding of the influences which make it so beautiful, combining the farmer's instinctive feeling for the shape of the land with the artist's inner eye.

He has not only walked all these routes and checked them with the Peak Park Planning Board but, where they cross open country on access land, he has consulted landowners for, as a farmer himself, he understands better than many in the walking fraternity the problems faced by farmers.

I warmly commend this book as an outstanding footpath guide which will provide walkers with endless pleasure.

Hugh Westacott
Adstock, Buckingham
June 1982

ACKNOWLEDGEMENTS

I would like to express my gratitude to Mike Ingham (Access Officer) and Harry Jones (Footpath Officer) on the staff of the Peak Park at Aldern House, who together with Ken Drabble, Mike Hammond, Ian Hurst, Brian Jones, Gordon Miller, and Peter McGowan (Park Rangers) have generously given me their attention and invaluable advice throughout the preparation of this guide.

In addition I greatly appreciate the contact with tenant farmers, water board officials and other interested local people, from the concern and inter-relationship of such people has come a deeper personal understanding of the High Peak as a place of work and recreation.

I also wish to thank Iain Liddell who cast a keen eye over the text, rectifying my faltering pen. A special thanks is due to Rodney Busby who together with Ben and Tim Roberts have on various occasions accompanied me and cheered my step.

But most of all I thank my dear wife Helen, for patience and understanding beyond the call of duty throughout those long deskbound months.

INTRODUCTION

This guide is the first part of a two volume survey designed to balance the marvellous diversity and wealth of walking country contained in the Peak District National Park.

High Peak Walks encompass the Dark Peak moors of Black Hill, Bleaklow, Kinder Scout, the higher eastern edges and the annexed western gritstone uplands from Windgather to The Roaches. A second volume will deal with the softer limestone region of the White or Low Peak.

The present area is characterised by great swelling moorland composed of sandstones and shales capped by a coarse gritstone, known as Millstone Grit, outcropping along plateau edges and scarps. Gritsone is pervious but a climatic quirk caused a thin impervious sedimentation to stop water penetration and triggered the formation of a thick blanket of peat over the Pennine uplands. The process is now subject to rapid degeneration caused by numerous agencies including climatic change, air pollution, fire, over-grazing and regretfully excessive localised recreational use. This ecological decline may have cyclical characteristics, but the present rate of erosion is little short of alarming, threatening not just the visual charm of the moors, but more insidious, their future economic values.

Twenty-two day-long circular walks and one linear challenge walk, carefully researched and described, offer walkers a practical and entertaining means of acquainting themselves with this popular moorland region. Each walk is designed to embrace particular localities, drawing on the contrasting qualities of each to sustain interest and develop an appreciation of the wild, dramatic and often shy beauty peculiar to this northern sector of Peakland. As circular walks they comply to no rigid form, walkers being at liberty to embellish the routes to suit their own inclinations, mindful of the terms and bounds of Access Land with the further obligation to use only Access Points when entering or leaving Access Land.

The walks are a fine initiation to the delights of moorland walking and for the normally active person should pose few problems in fair weather. Inclement weather and in particular dense clinging mist, coupled with the arduous peat groughs, can draw deeply into the resources and competence of any walker. Attention to compass work is of critical importance and cannot be over-emphasised; intuition and a feel for the lie of the land, have no place upon the featureless wilderness of Kinder, Bleaklow or Black Hill.

No walker should venture forth without equipping him or herself with reserves of high energy food and adequate waterproof clothing, keep a weather eye and prepare for the worst even when all seems settled. It would be prudent to study 'Safety on Mountains', an immensely practical booklet produced by the British Mountaineering Council.

The maps in this guide are founded on the Ordnance Survey I : 25,000 series, but are not intended as substitutes. I would seriously advise walkers to carry the 1" Tourist Map of the Peak District from which to take surer bearings. The 2½" Outdoor Leisure maps 'Dark Peak' and 'White Peak' are first rate productions upon which walkers can rely and represent the best general basis for planning and executing walks and expeditions.

Prescribing specific walking routes can have detrimental effects by concentrating walkers on paths that are already subject to heavy use. The lateral exaggeration of paths is becoming an acute and unsightly problem, notably on stretches of the Pennine Way. However, walkers will always be attracted to the scenic and more dramatic places, so where possible sympathetic lines have been chosen to effect some alleviation.

The National Park Ranger Service through its direct action within the Park advising visitors (and guidebook writers!), its involvement in emergency and rescue operations, together with practical footpath maintenance and conservation work, are a necessary liaisonary constraint against the worst effects of the visitor influx.

The eighteenth century enclosures and subsequent development of grouse shooting during the nineteenth and early twentieth centuries transformed the vast tracts of waste heather and sphagnum moor into the sole preserve of game birds. This effectively denied the less privileged classes the simple liberty to enjoy the freedom and healthy exercise of roaming across the high moors that formed a backdrop to their daily labours. The exclusive rights claimed by the landowning aristocracy, enforced by gamekeepers, inevitably generated a ground swell of resentment. Local rambling opinion began to wage concerted action against what they felt was an unreasonable severance of ancient access rights.

This culminated in the National Parks and Access to the

Countryside Act, 1949 (amended by the Countryside Act, 1968) which empowered Local Authorites to make arrangements with landowners for the public to have access to open country. To date the Peak Park Joint Planning Board have secured some 76 square miles of High Peak moorland which is patrolled by full and part-time Rangers who endeavour to ensure that the public comply with the terms set out in the access agreements, Access Land covers large tracts of Kinder Scout, Bleaklow, Langsett, Longdendale and Chew Moors together with portions of Stanage, Froggatt, Curbar, Baslow and Birchen Edges. Furthermore, the Board has purchased Windgather Rocks and The Roaches Estate where it is imposing a firm management control by obliging walkers to keep to the rights of way and specific concessionary paths.

The National Park has powers to close any Access Land when prolonged periods of dry weather make catastrophic moorland fires likely. Public access is also withdrawn for a maximum of twelve weekdays during the grouse shooting season - 12th August - 10th December. In this latter case only clearly defined sections of moorlands are affected, ample notice is given of impending closure, such information being displayed on boards around the area and specifically on Access Points on the actual day - rights of way remain open at such times. The bye-laws affecting public behaviour on Access Land are displayed on the reverse of each Access Point signboard. Walkers should be mindful that from mid-April to mid-June moorland traverses can cause disturbance to nesting birds, especially grouse, which may result in the loss of chicks. In Spring and early Summer in-lamb ewes are particularly vulnerable to thoughtless disturbance: sheep-worrying has no seasonal preference which is why dogs must be on a lead at all times both on valley paths and when on open country Access Land.

It is important to stress that walkers are not at liberty to camp on any farmland or open country within the National Park without prior permission of the landowner, his agent or tenant. Certain farmers allow a certain degree of casual camping in the vicinity of the farm, but seldom grant it on open moor.

The Peak Park Board has made provision for campers by establishing small camp sites with good facilities at Fieldhead (Edale), Crowden, Bowden Bridge (Hayfield), North Lees Hall (Stanage), and Hagg Farm (adjacent to the Youth Hostel in the Woodlands Valley). Youth Hostellers are well blessed with accommodation, ten hostels coming within the High Peak bounds: Marsden, Langsett, Edale, Castleton, Hathersage, Windgather, Gradbach and Meerbrook. Additionally, Crowden and Hagg Farm Hostels are open to non-members being owned by the National Park Authority and run by the Y.H.A.

Presentation of the Walks

Each walk is mapped at the uniform scale of two inches to one mile and supported by a detailed route commentary. Visual support is given by a small skyline diagram which helps convey something of the overall form of the walk, whilst the gradient profile gives fair warning of the strenuous sections not immediately apparent from simply glancing at the map (mindful that the hags and groughs of the peat plateau can amply compensate for any lack of contours). Useful alternative routes are included on the maps which are otherwise specific to the needs of walkers primarily engaged in following the described walk. Line illustrations perform the role of highlighting principal features and panoramic details along the way.

Whilst I can understand the viewpoint that charges meticulous route description as an anathema to the precious spirit of free adventure, it is to be hoped that users of this guide will recognise its value as a stepping stone towards a rich treasury of personal discovery.

Mountain Rescue

Mountain Rescue services are co-ordinated by the Police through controllers nominated by the Peak District Mountain Rescue Organisation. If you require aid from the Rescue Services Dial 999 and ask for the Police Operations Room.

All walkers would be well advised to visit the National Park Information Centre at Edale, preferably before venturing into the hills for the first time. There is a static exhibition vividly explaining the life and character of the Dark Peak together with warnings about the grough landscape, bringing into sharp focus the problems walkers must be prepared to face. Too many people set out into the hills ill-equipped thereby putting at risk their own lives and those of volunteer Rescue Teams. The Information Centre staff are only too pleased to offer advice and guidance. A range of informative and practical advice leaflets are available at the desk together with more substantive publications and Park management study reports.

Information

Whilst every effort has been made to verify the information in this book, neither the author nor publisher can accept responsibility for errors or omissions. Details change with time and the author would be pleased to receive any written corrections, impressions or ideas from readers. Letters should be addressed to the author via the publisher.

The peat landscape of Kinder Scout

MAP SYMBOLS

as used on the large scale route maps

Described walk ⌇⌇⌇⌇⌇

Match asterisks for route continuation ∗∗∗

Other visible paths or tracks ⌇⌇⌇⌇

Distance from starting point ⑦

Trees   Direction of North

Wall ━━━━ Broken wall •••••••• Fence ━━━━━

Buildings ▪▪ Church + Youth Hostel ▲

Tumulus ✳ Crags ᨓᨓᨓ Boulders ⋰⋱

Triangulation column △ Prominent cairn ▵

Access Point to Open Country ▼

Contours graduated at 100' intervals   700 600 500

Stream or River (arrow indicates direction of flow)

Waterfall ⋎ Footbridge ⤳   MRP/K :

Marshy ground ⋎⋎⋎   Mountain Rescue Post or Kit

Major road ━━━━━━━━━━━━━━

Minor road ━━━━━━━━━━━━━━

Other road ═══════════════

Railway ━━━━━━━━━━━━━━

Chapter One

For walkers engaged on the Pennine Way the traverse of Black Hill is seen as an uncharitable, unforgiving and thoroughly disagreeable moorland obstacle. Those sullen hordes thereby do a disservice not merely to its pathways but also its public image. To gain meaningfully from any walk upon its expansive wet shoulders and deep lonely cloughs a more flexible attitude of discovery is needed.   The three walks that follow offer the walker an intimacy and perspective that the heavily laden backpacker with his mind fixed on Malham and Hadrian's Wall, cannot know. The Pennine Way gains no space in this guide: it is, in the context of this book, an anti-Peakland walk bounding irresistably northward - albeit into the chest high bogs on White Moss!

A pinnacle on Great
Dovestone Rocks
WALK TWO

GRADIENT PROFILE
of
WALK
2

2

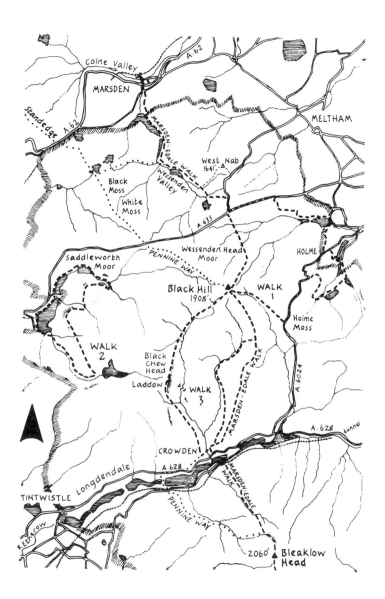

WALK 1

from Digley Reservoir

BLACK HILL

10¾ miles

Black Hill is a much maligned tract of wild moorland, composed largely of poor plant species and a rapidly eroding peat horizon, the kind of place to visit once, as so many Pennine Wayfarers are obliged to do, and leave to the whispering wind. The summit is a sorry quagmire of pudding peat, deprived of vegetative cover by the all too frequent moorland fires.

Yet the massif does have many virtues, as the three walks in this book will show. This walk is largely a Yorkshire affair, indeed much of the higher reaches of Black Hill are tenanted by Holme valley farmers. The route goes up Marsden Clough and onto the Holmfirth road proceeding beyond the site of the Isle of Skye Hotel before plunging headlong onto the Pennine Way alternative going above Issue Clough to the summit. Thereafter the walk markedly improves via Heyden Head and the Holme Moss road. Descending toward Holme a forestry track curves round into the pleasant environs of Holmfirth Woods where four reservoirs are inspected prior to passing up through the village of Holme en route back to Digley Reservoir.

Emley Moor I.B.A. Mast

Holmfirth Woods and Yateholm Reservoir from the Holme Moss pass

4

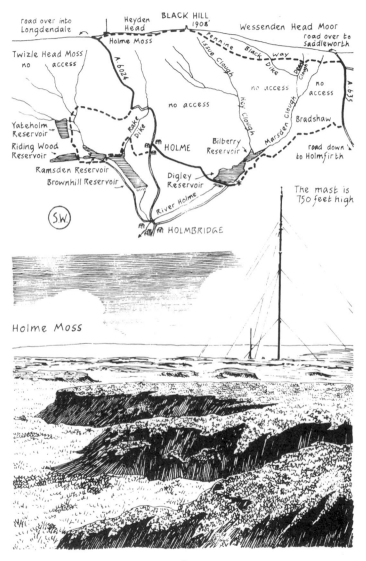

road over into
Longdendale

Heyden
Head

BLACK HILL
1908'

Wessenden Head Moor
road over to
Saddleworth

Holme Moss

Twizle Head Moss
no access

Pennine Black Way

Issue Clough

Dike

no access

A 6024

no access

Yateholm
Reservoir

Riding Wood
Reservoir

Rake Dike

Hey Clough

Marsden Clough

Dean Clough

A 635

Bradshaw

HOLME

Bilberry
Reservoir

road down
to Holmfirth

Ramsden Reservoir

Brownhill Reservoir

Digley
Reservoir

S.W.

River Holme

HOLMBRIDGE

Holme Moss

The mast is
750 feet high

5

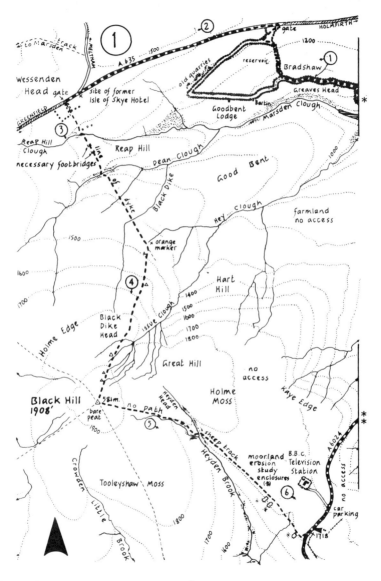

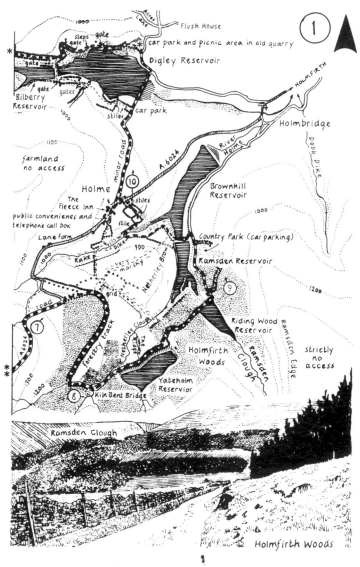

Access Lane

Flush House

car park and picnic area in old quarry

Digley Reservoir

steps gate
gate
gate

HOLMFIRTH

Bilberry Reservoir

gate
gates

stiles

car park

Holmbridge

1000

River Holme

Dobb Dike

1100

farmland no access

minor road

A 6024

Brownhill Reservoir

1000

Holme

10

The Fleece Inn

stiles

public convenienes and telephone call box

stile

Country Park (car parking)

Lane Farm

Dike

Rake

900

Ramsden Reservoir

very marshy

grid

Netherley Brook

9

1100

1000

road

7

forestry track

Netherley Clough

Dobb Edge

Riding Wood Reservoir

Ramsden Edge

Holmfirth Woods

Ramsden Clough

strictly no access

1200

1300

1200

Holmfirth Woods

Yateholm Reservoir

8

Kiln Bent Bridge

Ramsden Clough

Holmfirth Woods

If, upon arrival at Digley, you discover that dear old Black Hill is obliterated by an intractable mass of low cloud, take heart, bless the Yorkshire Water Authority and the men who created Don Forest, their endeavours have revitalised the sombre flanks of these Pennine moors, the day need not be a total loss, take the opportunity to discover the six beautiful reservoirs, a sanctuary for much wild life, amid the luxuriant mixed forestry of Holmfirth Woods. But when parking your car please put it in either of the Digley dam parks or at the Ramsden Country Park, not in Holme. In mist Black Hill should be left well alone.

The walk :

Let's imagine that the sun really is shining, as indeed it did on one of my numerous forays from the Holme valley, and head for Black Hill with spirits high. From Digley the most prominent feature on the skyline is the B.B.C. transmitter mast, yet whilst the mountain may lack exciting natural features from this aspect it does still manage to impose a strong presence upon the locality making it a worthy objective.

Leave the quarry picnic site by the lane westward, a submerged section deflecting the lakeside path into the adjacent pasture by a gate, right. Continue down a flight of steps soon rejoining the lane through a gate. The walled lane proceeds above Bilberry Reservoir, today a placid sheet of water but remembered locally still with emotion for its brutal ferocity, for in February 1852, long before Digley dam was raised, Bilberry dam collapsed emptying 90 million gallons of water down the Holme valley, within half an hour, causing colossal destruction and the loss of 81 lives. Raise your head to the hills and be mindful of the respect every mountain deserves, they may be fun to climb but they are not totally passive giants.   Watch for the branch right up what appears to be a walled stream course, just short of Bartin (barn). Keen eyed map readers will have noticed a footpath proceeding beyond Goodbent Lodge via Reap Hill Clough to the `Isle of Skye', but respecting the wishes of the tenant farmer I am not recommending its use.

 The mile or so of broad verged highway, followed from the gate above Bradshaw, may not be everyone's idea of delightful walking but enjoy the firm tread while you may for things will soon be very different! For, just beyond the site of the Isle of Skye Hotel (opposite the Meltham road junction), the real business of the day is commenced. Many Peakland treks have ended or begun from this spot, the Bog Dodgers Way passes this way, as do well advised Pennine Way hikers avoiding the dreadful bogs on White Moss.

8

The path leading down to Reap Hill Clough though well trod is quite firm, however, the succeeding stretch to Dean Clough is not so well favoured, the blanket peat being so badly worn that two crude footbridges have been erected to span bad spots, but to adequately cope with all the mire one single span from Reap Hill Clough to Issue Clough would be necessary, something of a nonsense! Dean Clough has cut a deep and rocky course and calls for steady footwork. Beyond, the path maintains its south-easterly course following what appears to be a boundary dyke of uncertain age. It is interesting to note that these waters, Dean Clough, Black Dike and so on, flow into Marsden Clough which itself means 'boundary valley', any connection? At the orange gas pipe marker the dyke is forsaken, right (the rising path may not be the strict right-of-way, but the farmer prefers that walkers adhere to one route and this is more likely to occur if it is also the common way). The path mounts steadily with the occasional random cairn for guidance, through the groughs at the head of Issue Clough, eventually to stumble upon the Ordnance Survey column on the Soldiers Lump. This is the equally appropriate alternative name for the summit of Black Hill, for the entire summit plateau is akin to the aftermath of trench warfare, the legacy of recent peat fires started it can only be surmised by careless walkers. When frozen or bone dry the going is pleasant, when wet the oozing peat does not engender a desire to halt, which is just as well as there is no view worth the name from this bleak vantage. Whether misty or clear, wet or dry, I would earnestly advise all walkers take a precise compass bearing on the watersmeet in upper Heyden Brook; this gets you off the peaty wastes swiftly and once the stream is crossed a pronounced sheep track leads gently up towards the A.6024 road. On course for the road, keeping nicely under the hag fringe, three small enclosures are passed, their purpose being to examine the effects of non-interference on the eroding edges of the plateau. The last one has been colonised by heather, a plant conspicuous by its absence elsewhere in the vicinity. The lessons of this broad survey and study clearly need to be heeded if vegetation is to exist on the high Pennines. If you choose to plod round Heyden Head and across Holme Moss to pass the transmitting station do beware if icy conditions prevail as the stabilising cables can shed lethal doses of ice upon the unwary. The moorland stage is now concluded upon joining the road, it is, however, to be hoped that someday walkers may enjoy a relaxation of the access restrictions sealing off Twizle Head and Ramsden Clough, thereby bringing this excursion to its more natural conclusion. Reluctantly the walk must quit the high ground down the A.6024 road, which is liable to partial closure occasioned by subsidence. The view down into Holmfirth Woods and north-eastwards over the rolling west facing scarpland landscape featuring the Emley Moor mast which stands some five miles south east of Huddersfield being the one saving grace of this enforced retreat.

The route leaves the road at the sharp lefthand bend proceeding down a rough lane to join a forestry track, turning right. This track leads round under the embankment of Yateholm Reservoir. A substantial community of scattered farmsteads once existed in this area; today this is a place to stroll, to observe the flight of birds and the passage of clouds and muse on life. Soon the track becomes a surfaced road crossing Riding Wood dam with its impressive backdrop of Ramsden Edge. Ramsden Clough is a jealously guarded grouse preserve and walkers must respect the landowners wishes. By excluding the general public from this dramatic valley head one vital pocket of healthy moor may persist, someday this too will fall to access probably at the desinence of the grouse shoot. The road goes round above Ramsden Reservoir to the Country Park, the popular resort of locals and day-trippers. Walkers may care to explore the footpaths in this locality, of those plotted on my map those by Rake Dike and Netherley Clough are to be recommended and give an interesting circuit via Holme village from this Country Park.

To continue, go left, to cross Ramsden dam in the 'cage walk' then steeply up a muddy path. Round a spur descend to the enchanting Rake Dike footbridge in a setting of embowered waterfalls. Again the path climbs steeply to a stile, crosses a small paddock turning left over a double stile to follow the wall into Holme. Entering the village curiosity will be roused by the aptly named futuristic abode 'Underhill'. The architect owner Arthur Quarmby has contrived a functional yet cunningly camouflaged house, with dome skylights to capture an even spread of light internally, with both a garden and swimming pool built-in - why are not more houses built on this ingenious mole principle effectively merging into the landscape. Holme is a place for pioneers. Indeed it can boast to have been the first community in Yorkshire to generate its own electricity, it once thrived through a combination of farming and weaving, the cottage woollen industry persisting here until the 1890's.

Walkers may choose to visit the Fleece Inn to partake of local conviviality before departing down the minor road from the old Sunday School, noting the carved directive hands pointing to Woodhead (via Holme Moss) and down to Holmfirth. Attention is drawn to the holes at the top of the dry-stone walls flanking this lane. There are twenty-five pairs into which were once slotted tenter hooks upon which yarn was spread to dry, a fascinating survival from this lost local industry. The lane descends to cross the Digley dam, though with energy to spare you may conclude the expedition by doing a full tour of the reservoir.

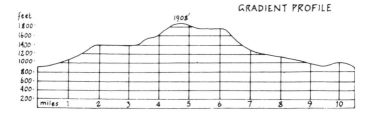

GRADIENT PROFILE

feet
1800
1600
1400
1200
1000
800
600
400
200

1908'

miles 1 2 3 4 5 6 7 8 9 10

10

Ramsden Reservoir

Holme Moss from Netherley Clough

WALK 2   THE SADDLEWORTH EDGES

Dovestone Reservoir and Wimberry Rocks

from Binn Green   8¾ miles

This second expedition on the Black Hill massif must rank as one
of the best in northern Peakland, a veritable feast for the eyes: here are
deep valleys rimmed with bold craggy edges and three silver sheets of
water fill the vale with one set high upon the moor for good
measure.   This is one of the walks that stands out in my memory
and I certainly look forward with relish to renewing my acquaintance
with this delectable corner of the Peak Park.

   For the people of Oldham these Saddleworth hills represent the
entire English Lake District encapsulated and transported to their
doorstep for their exclusive recreation and delight.   Trippers flock
to the Goyt Valley for an eighth of this grandeur (and a blessing too for
quite enough journey here).   The greatest blessing is that whilst so many
throng the Dovestone dam and Binn Green parks and stroll beside
the lakes, only a fraction climb the heights so the glorious parade
from Ravenstones to the Dish Stone may be accomplished in peace.
The edge walk would be made complete if it were possible to continue by
the Wilderness and Wimberry Moss to terminate at Alphin Pike, but
whilst this section comes within the National Park, it presently languishes
outside of access and must not be traversed without prior permission
from the landowners, the Stalybridge Estate - please heed!

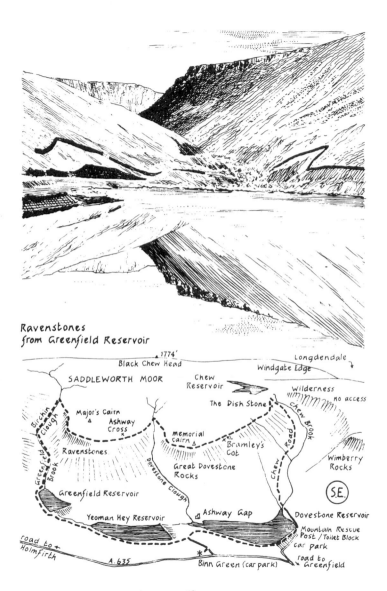

Ravenstones
from Greenfield Reservoir

▲ 1774'
Black Chew Head

Longdendale

Windgate Edge

SADDLEWORTH MOOR

Chew
Reservoir

Wilderness

no access

The Dish Stone

Chew Brook

Major's Cairn

Ashway
Cross

memorial
cairn ▲

Bramley's
Cot

Ravenstones

Great Dovestone
Rocks

Brichin Clough

Greenfield Brook

Dovestone Clough

Chew Road

Wimberry
Rocks

S.E.

Greenfield Reservoir

Ashway Gap

Yeoman Hey Reservoir

Dovestone Reservoir

road to
Holmfirth

A.635

Mountain Rescue
Post / Toilet Block
car park

★

Binn Green (car park)

road to
Greenfield

13

The Walk :

The Binn Green picnic area is a marvellous coign of vantage from which to comprehend the full stature of the Saddleworth theatre of hills and lakes. Reservoirs are invariably obtrusive but whereas in many instances they spell a death to charm, here their presence is creative. Some may even proclaim them a stunning accompaniment to the proud bluffs of gritstone rising above the watery depths.

From the toilet block descend a flight of steps to a stile into mid-growth conifers, the well used path leading down to a wall squeeze stile and onto the reservoir access road. Turn left, descend to the Yeoman Hey dam there branching left along the broad track beside the reservoir (which was built in 1880 to satisfy the industrial thirst of Oldham). The conifer plantation, Bill o'Jack's, above the track, bears the nickname of a former inn-keeper William Bradbury of the Moor Cock Inn which stood until 1935 by the Holmfirth road. He and his father John (Jack) met a tragic death at the hands of some unproven assailant/s in 1832 and were buried with much local sympathy at Saddleworth Church. The path rises with the relief channel to skirt Greenfield Reservoir (built in 1903), the latter part of the reservoir track proceeding in mesopotamian fashion, between waters, as ahead the stern cliffs of Ravenstones frown down upon the narrowing clough. The track, now much rougher, goes beside Greenfield Brook tumbling in a wild defile, the prefect setting for an ambush! High to the right note the split arête on the skyline. This is the Trinnacle, the most remarkable feature of this edge. Short of the clough divide, the track goes above the sinister entrance to the ¾ mile long aqueduct that captures the waters of Birchin Clough and sends them helter skelter down the tunnel shoot into Dovestone Reservoir. On no account venture into this fearful black hole. Cross to the far bank of Birchin Clough and scramble up this delightful boulder strewn ravine, rock hopping amid stirring scenes of cascading water.

Major's cairn above Ravenstones

14

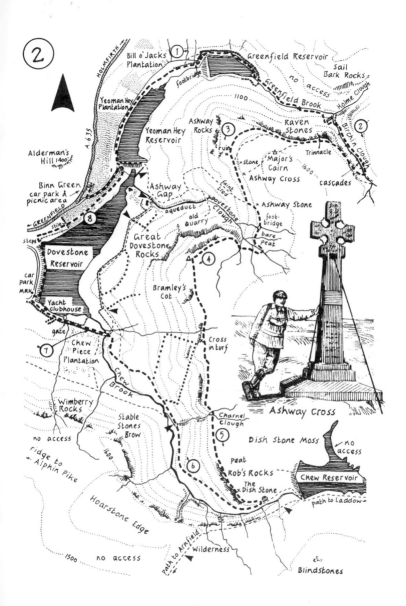

②

HOLMFIRTH

Bill o'Jacks Plantation ①

Greenfield Reservoir

Sail Bark Rocks

Yeoman Hey Plantation

footbridge

Greenfield Brook

no access

Holme Clough

1100

Yeoman Hey Reservoir

Ashway Rocks ③

ruin

Raven Stones

Birchin Clough

②

A 635

Alderman's Hill 1400

stone

Major's Cairn

Trinnacle

1600

Binn Green car park & picnic area

GREENFIELD

stile

⑧

Ashway Gap

aqueduct

old Quarry

Ashway Cross

faint trod

Dovestone Clough

cascades

Ashway Stone

footbridge

bare peat

steps

Dovestone Reservoir

Great Dovestone Rocks

④

car park MRK

Yacht clubhouse

gate

⑦

Chew Piece Plantation

Bramley's Cot

Cross in turf

Wimberry Rocks

Chew Brook

no access

ridge to Alphin Pike

Stable Stones Brow

1500

Charnel Clough

⑤

Dish Stone Moss

no access

Chew Reservoir

Hoarstone Edge

⑥

peat

Rob's Rocks

The Dish Stone

path to Laddow

1500

no access

path to Arnfield

Wilderness

Blindstones

Ashway Cross

15

Birchin Clough

Alderman Hill from Greenfield Reservoir

Ravenstones

The Trinnacle, Ravenstones

Above the cascades, find a convenient fording point and make your way cautiously up the steep hillside to reach the brow, there joining a clear edge path leading to the pronounced rock prow overlooking the confluence of Birchin Clough with Holme Clough, which drains the spongy wastes of Black Hill. On the opposing hillside a small rock wall is seen, this is Sail Bark Rocks and in common with all the facing moor access is strictly forbidden. The wild scene has strong overtones of some remote glen, indeed, it is not hard to imagine golden eagles quartering the sky, as they did here until the early 19thC. Time can be well spent here admiring the superb rock architecture particularly the Trinnacle. The red-blooded among the party may deem the profound drop no deterrent to standing on top of this perilously exposed pinnacle - as did the obliging Voluntary Ranger in my drawing!

A choice of three routes lead to the Ashway Cross, that by Major's cairn is the thinnest path. Major was a dog in whose company his owner often wandered upon these edges and moors, the name of this much loved canine companion is inscribed frequently about the Ravenstones locality. The large cairn, illustrated on the previous page is not visible from the edge path, though it may be espied from the Holmfirth road above Bill o'Jack's.

The main route swings round the edge above Ashway Rocks and past the Platt Memorial (Ashway Cross) and Ashway Stone, an isolated natural rock table. The broad path contours round to the head of Dovestone Clough, with clear evidence of marginal peat erosion to hamper progress, fording above the upper cascade. The old beater's trod returns to the rocky edge above Great Dovestone Rocks with glorious views to heighten the pleasure. The path now reaches the prominent memorial cairn, overlooking Dovestone Reservoir (a fine spot to stop for a snack) note Alderman Hill rising above Binn Green and the obelisk at Pots and Pans. The edge route heads due south, passing Bramley's Cot, an ingenious and obviously sturdy dwelling, a monument in its own right to its builders, though it is not clear what purpose it served (shepherd's summer abode?).The peaty margin is followed beyond Charnel Clough to the Dish Stone. On the opposing hillside is Wilderness Gully, where in 1963 an avalanche, reputedly the biggest recorded in England, swept two local climbers to their death. Beyond, the ridge continues via Stable Stones to the prominent Wimberry Rocks, deemed the best climbers crag in the Saddleworth locality. The walk descends beside an old quarry cut to provide dam material for Chew Reservoir. This lonely sheet of water is worth a glance for at 1600ft. it is the highest constructed reservoir in England (built in 1912). The road built to service the reservoir offers a swift descent with good views ahead and of the enclosing walls to the Chew valley at either hand. The track improves lower down and approaching the Chew Brook bridge a path branching right may be followed to Binn Green via Ashway Gap House. However, more pleasantly the main route proceeds past the sailing club to diverge onto the dam walkway, following the well marked path back to Yeoman Hey.

The Dish Stone
looking west

Bramley's Cot

Cairn above Great Dovestone Rocks
with tablet " In memory of Brian Toase
17-8-1949 — 18-8-1972 and Tom Morton
16-10-1950 — 18-8-1972 who lost their lives
whilst descending the second
Sella Tower, Italian Dolomites."

WALK 3   BLACK HILL

from Crowden

8½ miles

To think that once Crowden was a lively, active, community
with several pubs and a fine Hall and in its way productive
serving an important trade route into Yorkshire whilst having
a significant agrarian existence. The traveller today sees little
worthy of those past days, so much change has befallen the valley.
Inevitably the one sure resource of this locality is rainwater, as many
wretched Pennine wayfarers can testify, so all else has been
sacrificed to ensure a good supply of pond filler. However, I
cannot say that all is negative and dismal: indeed, having spent a
week exploring the various walk options on Black Hill, and only once
in wet conditions, I have a fair measure of affection for these moors
and in particular for Laddow which alone would justify setting out
on this excursion

The walk :

At Crowden there is a hostel and a light-weight camping site serving
Pennine Way folk and a newly created car parking area adjacent to
the hostel from where this walk springs.

Proceed along the walled lane, once the main thoroughfare, branching
right along the track to Rotherham Outdoor Centre, turning right again
short of the bridge. A cobbled track zig-zags on course for Brockholes
Quarry, but walkers must follow the open country signs up the steep and
eroding path beside the wall left, going beneath the huge tip of Loftend
Quarry. At the broken cross wall open country is entered, soon after
this the path forks, retain the lower line and go with this delightful
old shooters track right up the valley at the gentlest of gradients.

In winter this valley is a fine place to observe the mountain hare, the way
is also a soothing prelude to the more physical exchanges necessary to cope
with the notorious raw peat on the higher plateau. The Crowden Little
Brook valley narrows and curves then approaching a sheepfold the path runs
its course. Originally a shooting cabin stood here but all trace has now
gone, hereon only the stream itself assists navigation there being no path.
If a mist closes in at this point and your will to reach the summit exceeds
your good sense to retreat set your course to Black Hill by the brook. But
in fair weather it is preferable to diverge to the pronounced shoulder of Tooleyshaw Moor, and follow the broad ridge top path threading through the hags.
Shortly after the three mile point to one's amazement the ridge is totally
bereft of peat: a dreadful legacy from a peat fire that smouldered for
many months. The bed rock is succeeded by raw peat as you close in on the summit.

20

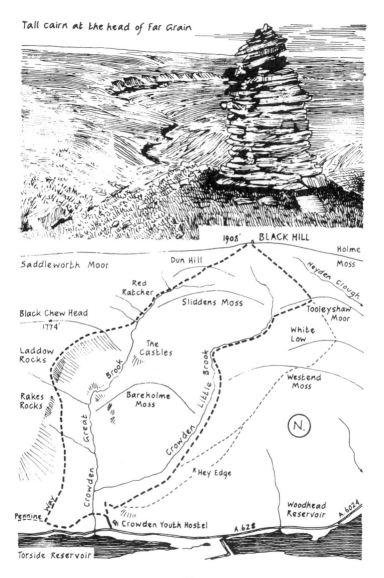

Tall cairn at the head of Far Grain

1908' BLACK HILL

Holme Moss

Saddleworth Moor

Dun Hill

Heyden Clough

Red Ratcher

Sliddens Moss

Tooleyshaw Moor

Black Chew Head
1774'

The Castles

White Low

Laddow Rocks

Brook

Crowden Little Brook

Westend Moss

Rakes Rocks

Bareholme Moss

N.

Great

Crowden

Hey Edge

Pennine Way

Crowden

Woodhead Reservoir

A.6024

Crowden Youth Hostel

A.628

Torside Reservoir

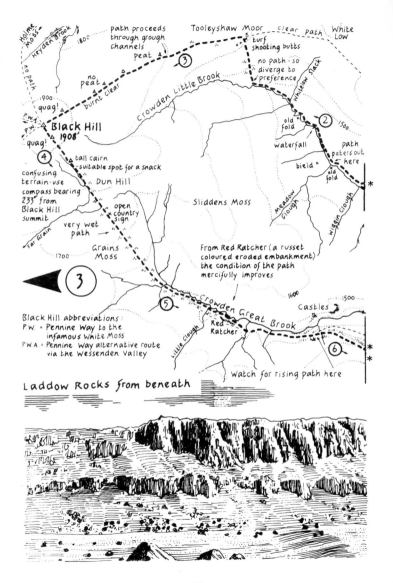

path proceeds
through grough
channels
peat

Tooleyshaw Moor ---- clear path ---- White
Low

turf
shooting butts

③

no path - so
diverge to
preference

Holme Moss

Heyden Brook

1800

no path

no
peat

burnt clear

1900
quag!

Crowden Little Brook

Whitelow Slack

P.W.
P.W.

Black Hill
1908'

quag!

old
fold

②

1500

④

tall cairn
suitable spot for a snack

Dun Hill

waterfall

bield

old
fold

path
peters out
here

*

confusing
terrain - use
compass bearing
233° from
Black Hill
summit

open
country
sign

Sliddens Moss

Meadow Clough

Wiggin Clough

*

Far Grain

very wet
path →

1700

Grains
Moss

From Red Ratcher (a russet
coloured eroded embankment)
the condition of the path
mercifully improves

1600

1500

Castles

◀ ③

⑤

Crowden Great Brook

Black Hill abbreviations:
P.W. = Pennine Way to the
infamous White Moss
P.W.A = Pennine Way alternative route
via the Wessenden Valley

Little Clough

Red
Ratcher

⑥

*
*

Watch for rising path here

Laddow Rocks from beneath

22

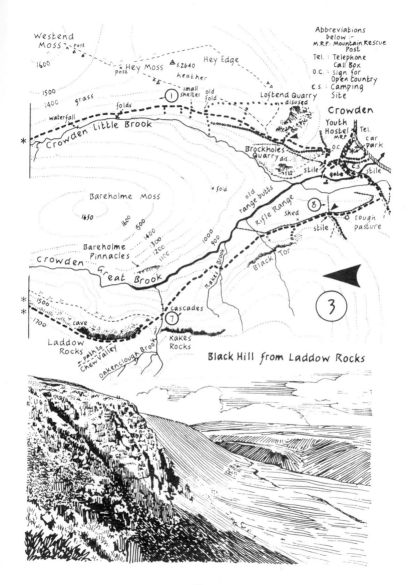

Abbreviations below :-
M.R.P. : Mountain Rescue Post
Tel. : Telephone Call Box
O.C. : sign for Open Country
C.S. : Camping Site

Westend Moss
post
1600
Hey Moss
post
Hey Edge
heather
△ s.2640
1500
1400
grass
folds
small shelter
old fold
Loftend Quarry
disused
waterfall
Crowden Little Brook
Crowden
Youth Hostel
Tel.
M.R.P.
car Park
O.C.
Brockholes Quarry dis.
stile
gate
C.S.
stile

Bareholme Moss
1450
1600
1500
fold
old range butts
Rifle Range
shed
8
1400
1300
1200
1100
1000
900
stile
rough pasture

Bareholme Pinnacles
Crowden Great Brook
Raven Brook
Black Tor

3

1500
1700
cave
cascades
7
Laddow Rocks
path to Chew Valley
Oakenclough Brook
Kakes Rocks

Black Hill from Laddow Rocks

23

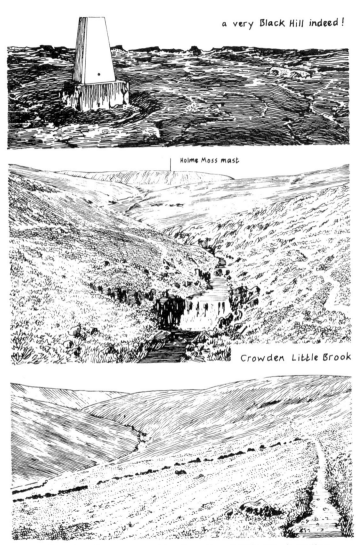

a very Black Hill indeed!

Holme Moss mast

Crowden Little Brook

Shooter's path advancing up the Crowden Little Brook Valley

Climbers' cave beneath the northern buttress of Laddow Rocks

Today the O.S. column (s.2958) languishes not on a firm oasis of turf, as it was the day Alfred Wainwright passed this way in the mid 1960's, the enveloping quagmire being now complete. It can be a mindless habit that when actually ontop of your mountain you toss down your pack, relax and consume some portion of your rations. Such an activity is wholly undesirable here, so proceed on a compass bearing of 233° to reach the tall cairn above Far Grain (illustrated above the route diagram), where the necessary couch awaits.

This dry spot on Holme Edge is also a far better viewpoint from which to gaze across the broad expanse of Saddleworth Moor to Black Chew Head, Laddow and Bleaklow seen over Sliddens Moss. Take the opportunity to examine the next stage of the route - beware! do not just wander down the clough thinking this to be the headwaters of Crowden Great Brook for infact you will end up admiring Ravenstones in walk 2 crossing non-access land in the process and be far from happy about the prospect of adding the miles up Chew Brook to Laddow. So hold onto that compass bearing which is fixed on the watersmeet in upper Crowden Great Brook. From Dun Hill to Red Ratcher it is marshy every step of the way and no bee-line is possible despite the basically level surface. Fording the brook twice beneath Red Ratcher the going is markedly better and the walker may bound along above the deepening ravine. Pay attention as the path comes onto steeper ground approaching the Castles, the somewhat indefinite divergence of the Laddow high-level route which, in all but the severest weather, must be adopted.

The Castles

Oakenclough Brook

Crowden Great Brook

View downdale from Rakes Brook

Hey Edge

Loftend Quarry

Brockholes Quarry

The reason for this advice is that since so many fleet-footed Pennine Wayfarers have sped along the lower route beneath the crags to and from Oakenclough Brook the path thus formed appears as an ugly stain across the moor both aesthetically and ecologically undesirable. So do take the trouble to stay along the crest for the breath taking prospect from the crag top is in any case probably the highlight of this walk.

Laddow has one great weakness affecting both walkers and climbers in that because it is buttressed close into the peat moor this has the dual defect of permitting a continual flushing down the face, with peat and grit filling the handholds, and denying an easy appraisal of the cliff features from above. My advice, if slipping over the brink is to be avoided, is to clamber down the stony rake at the north end of the outcrop veering right below the cave to follow the undulations of the climbers traverse, thereby peering up at the many arêtes, cracks and chimneys that have throughout this century lured the boldest climbers by the sheer exhilarating quality of the many high standard routes. Retrace your steps by the cave rake and look abroad, northwards the moorland swells to form Black Hill and southward the long, unbroken skyline of Bleaklow fills the gulf. Far below, unseen and little suspected, Crowden Great Brook careers through a fierce ravine. This is an important and sensitive natural refuge and sanctuary, preferably left alone - please do not enter. ——→

The trail back down to Crowden could be, and probably has been, accomplished by a blind man, though the scenic pleasures notably the beautiful cascades in Oakenclough, make it preferable to more than feel the worn path beneath one's feet! Walkers whose appetites for these moors admit **no bounds may** retain the edge above Oakenclough and Rakes Rocks treading the grough margins to Highstones or even round to Lad's Leap, rejoining the main route at mile eight.

GRADIENT PROFILE

feet
1800·
1600·
1400·
1200·

1905'

1 2 3 4 5 6 7 8

Chapter Two

Bleaklow is not an easy mountain to get to know, for although it does flaunt its northern shoulders to casual observers in Longdendale, from all other angles it distances itself most effectively. It is often stated that the Pennine Way is let off lightly in its crossing of Bleaklow, though many would dispute that the raw peat between Alport Low and Bleaklow Head has few peers in the 'slough of despond' stakes. More accurately, the Pennine Way sees barely a fraction of the moorland's merits, as walkers who take the trouble to sample the set of walks in this chapter will surely aver. Each outing addresses a quite different aspect and combination of facets of the mountain and in consequence they draw out much of the Bleaklow mystique.

The Anvil, Bleaklow Stones

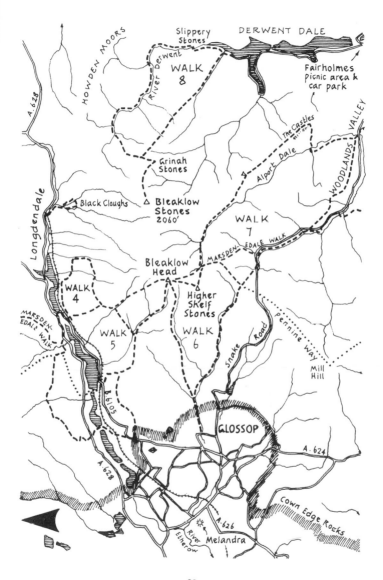

WALK 4 THE LONGDENDALE EDGES
from Crowden
12½ miles

Passing through Longdendale the traveller may be forgiven for dismissing the whole valley as forfeit to the necessities of our age. Disfigured though it may be, moments of high drama still exist as this excursion illustrates.   To appreciate the overriding beauty of Longdendale it is necessary to rise above the latter day impositions of industrial man and by gaining the craggy rim peer down and across at what still contrives to be a spacious and exciting progression along shattered rocky edges and by lonely heather moor.

Until 1974 Longdendale belonged to Cheshire, wedged between Derbyshire and Lancashire it projected a tenuous finger through to Yorkshire, being claimed for Cheshire by the first Earls of Chester who desired that their salt reach the important market that lay across the Pennines unhindered by intervening tolls and other trade restrictions.

Longdendale penetrates deep into the Pennine divide and must have served as a vital and direct east/west corridor for trade: indeed the discovery of Mesolithic (5,000 - 3,000 B.C.) chert weapons, from the Derbyshire Wye valley, clearly indicates its antiquity.

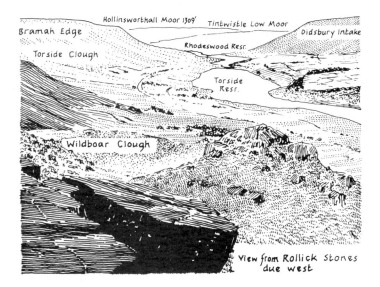

Hollinsworthall Moor 1309'   Tintwistle Low Moor
Bramah Edge   Didsbury Intake
Rhodeswood Resr.
Torside Clough
Torside Resr.
Wildboar Clough

View from Rollick Stones
due west

Torside Clough

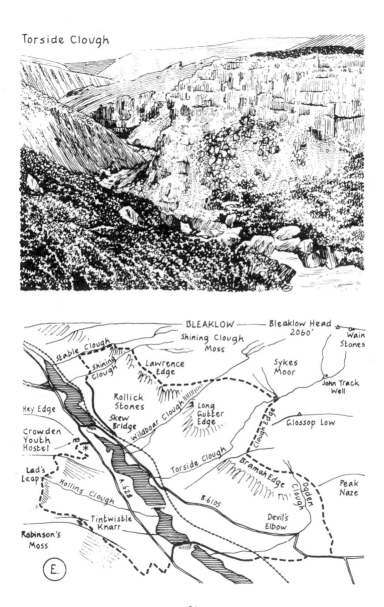

BLEAKLOW — Bleaklow Head 2060'
Wain Stones
Shining Clough Moss
Stable Clough
Shining Clough
Lawrence Edge
Sykes Moor
John Track Well
Rollick Stones
Wildboar Clough
Long Gutter Edge
Hey Edge
Skew Bridge
Clough Edge
Glossop Low
Crowden Youth Hostel
Torside Clough
Bramah Edge
Lad's Leap
Hollins Clough
A.628
Peak Naze
Ogden Clough
B.6105
Devil's Elbow
Tintwistle Knarr
Robinson's Moss

E.

The Walk :

Whilst there are plans to develop a country park on the southern side of Torside Reservoir the presently available, though limited capacity, car park adjacent to Crowden Youth Hostel is therefore to be recommended as the start point for this walk. Casual parking at Skew Bridge is not welcomed, please heed.

From the Hostel to the steps down to the Woodhead dam road there is mercifully a pavement. In a perfect world a footpath would strike out across the head of the Torside Reservoir enclosure short-cutting the walk to Skew Bridge. This enforced road trek which persists almost to The Lodge effectively takes away most of the monotony of unyielding tarmac at the very beginning of the day. Above the Woodhead dam standing in forlorn isolation, frowning disapproval upon all it now surveys, is St.James' Church. Like a candle in the wind, a defiant reminder that even since the Manchester Corporation flooded the green meadows of yore, creating the then largest expanse of artifical water in the world (between 1847 and 1870), there lingered some semblance of community life hereabouts. To all intents and purposes this is now extinguished, yet whilst the valley has value then the scattered handful of tenant farmers, watermen and others that remain may someday form the nucleus of a revival.

From Skew Bridge the route follows the private access road, past an old mill and some rather dilapidated railway cottages, towards The Lodge, diverging at the sign to Open Country. Follow the fence, skirt the pond, ford Shining Clough and contour beside the recently erected in-by fence to join the clear track that mounts above Stable Clough. Possibly this track was created to haul stone from the Edge and later found use as an approach for shooting parties. It is flanked by shooting butts (please respect all shooting butts, wherever found) and where it swings right towards Shining Clough Rocks (an optional route to the Edge for able scramblers or a brief diversion to admire the crags) a narrow but well maintained path continues up the steeply confined clough. Branch right, onto the heather moor, passing a line of turf butts, to gain the edge top path there on glancing at the grand prospect of Longdendale and to the noble crag below festooned with hard, yet sound, rock routes ; there is a pinnacle here standing several feet clear of the main face and a narrow projecting flake of unique and intimidating proportions, so do give some time to this fascinating place.

The route next veers left into the upper ravine of Shining Clough (see drawing) crossing the gently stepping stream well above the great fall that clearly denies an easy exit for walkers. The broken edge proceeds westward by Dowstone and Deer Knowl, both old names reflecting a long lost animal association. Eroded peat hags fringe the edge, an all too common circumstance that can be a nuisance in very wet conditions. The next high point is Rollick Stones, a more minor climbing ground but certainly a fine viewpoint (see drawing), the name is suggestive of some strange antic!

Of the three climbing areas on this northern flank of Bleaklow Shining Clough Rocks are pre-eminent, comprising a main face split into six well defined buttresses. The East Buttress by virtue of its height and steepness is considered to be the finest and most imposing gritstone buttress in the entire Bleaklow area. This is a prime climbing ground for the very best cragsmen.

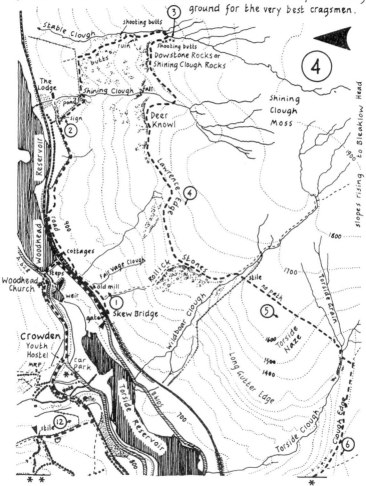

Wildboar Clough cuts a deep re-entrant into the Edge and the route goes in sympathy with the contours seeking a stile in the fence on the far bank. Scramblers delight at ascending this clough, within the fiendish cleft the water careers over a series of fierce rock steps, three of which require the skills and balance of seasoned rock hoppers. On no account contemplate a descent with the stream. Serious accidents here are regretfully too frequent, and it is far safer to retreat by either the Rollick Stones ridge or Fair Vage Clough.

Walkers can choose to wander with the Edge via Torside Naze but the going is not particularly pleasant under foot, so it is probably more satisfactory to take a bearing on the confluence of Torside Grain crossing the pathless heather moor. At the point of fording, Torside Clough is a narrow rockgirt moorland stream, but soon after the route has joined the Pennine Way to run along Clough Edge the clough expands into a giant amphitheatre, lined beneath the Edge by an exciting series of steep rock ribs and narrow buttresses, which have not been exhaustively climbed. The is a delightful advance with excellent views north to Black Hill.

As the Pennine Way begins to fall away towards Reaps, the Edges walk maintains height by Reaps Bent, following the path beside the fence along Bramah Edge. Can anyone explain this name? With no assistance from conventional sources I suggest "Broom well", bearing in mind that at the eastern end of Bleaklow "Grinah" means "the well of the grains." The route departs from the fence passing through a gateway in a broken cross wall then, swinging round the head of Ogden Clough under Peak Naze, it joins a track descending to a small conifer plantation, there passing round its northern edge to an access point stile onto the B.6105. Follow the road, right, to the bend where there is a stile on the left, descend the pastures to the railway underpass going through the succeeding paddock onto the lane leading down through Deepclough Farm to the Rhodeswood dam continuing up to meet the busy A.628.

The route crosses directly to an unusual turnstile then follows the track beside the wall branching right onto the zig-zagging quarrymens track. Entering Didsbury Intake through a gate, this currently is non-access land so pay attention to notices posted. The track mounts round the steep bluff to Tintwistle Knarr Quarry (Knarr itself means quarry), a considerable rock wall is on view, though no unauthorised climbing is permitted. Passing ruined gear a path rises to a stile by Rawkins Brook, proceeding by Black Gutter aiming for the post upon the skyline. From here follow the edge by Millstone Rocks to Lad's Leap. The name implies some super athletic feat though I have my doubts, the portals of Coombes Clough do not suggest such a possibility.

The way down to Crowden is straightforward, simply follow the well worn path to join the Pennine Way beneath Highstone Rocks. If time and energy permit, then following the peat passage skirt left along the hag margins of Span crossing the rim of Rake's Rocks to Oakenclough Brook, noted for its cascades, and thereafter climb to the top of Laddow Rocks - great stuff!

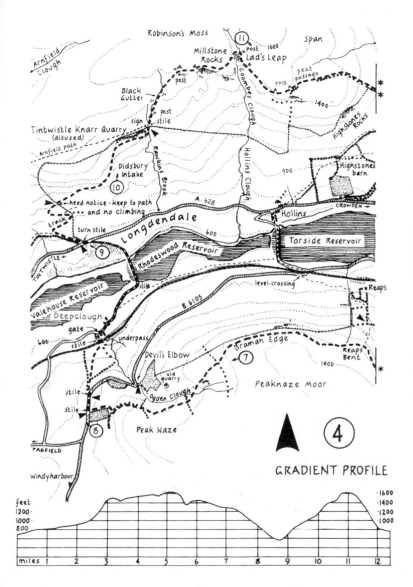

Robinson's Moss

Span

Arnfield Clough

⑪ Post 1600

Millstone Rocks

Lad's Leap

peat passage

post

post

1400

Highstones Rocks

Black Gutter

Coombes Clough

Hollins Clough

sign post stile

Tintwistle Knarr Quarry (disused)

Arnfield path

Rawkins Brook

900

Highstones barn

Didsbury Intake

⑩

heed notice · keep to path and no climbing

A.628

Hollins

CROWDEN

track

turn stile

Longdendale

600

Torside Reservoir

⑨

Rhodeswood Reservoir

TINTWISTLE

level-crossing

Reaps

Valehouse Reservoir

stile

B.6105

Deepclough

gate

stile

underpass

Devil's Elbow

Bramah Edge

Reaps Bent

600

old quarry

⑦

1400

stile

Ogden Clough

Peaknaze Moor

stile

⑧

Peak Naze

PADFIELD

▲ ④

Windyharbour

GRADIENT PROFILE

feet
1200
1000
800

·1600
·1400
·1200
·1000

miles 1 2 3 4 5 6 7 8 9 10 11 12

35

View down Shining Clough to Nine Holes Bridge

Woodhead Reservoir

Dowstone or Shining Clough Rocks

The Black Cloughs of Woodhead

Above the Woodhead Tunnel entrance cars may be parked and the plethora of insults to Longdendale's pride may be perused. Looking down dale ten high voltage pylons thread between the twin sweeps of the railway line and the Woodhead Reservoir. With this background a short exploration of the beautifully sylvan environs of the Black Cloughs comes as a pleasant contrast. The name Woodhead implies that at one time the upper Etherow valley had quite a considerable covering of trees, and whilst forestry plantings have made some recompense, the last vestige of natural woodland clings precariously to the steep cragbound lower flanks of the Black Cloughs.

From the car park descend the tunnel service road, cross the bridge then immediately left climb the stile beside the gate. A good track leads round into the light woodland beside the delightful boulder filled stream. Ford with care by the second shooting cabin then follow the thin undulating path keeping close to the stream. The frequent downpours that dose the Bleaklow plateau ensure a constant flow down these converging cloughs. After a particularly heavy period of rain the ravines echo to a thunderous roar and any attempt to ford the torrent would be extremely foolhardy. Proceeding up Middle Black Clough to the one major waterfall (a fine specimen it is too), the path takes avoiding action up the clearly easier lefthand side. From here you may choose either to stay

Middle Black Clough

within the clough or pursue the path along the rim amongst the dense heather growth. Many walkers choose this clough as their way of attaining Bleaklow Stones and certainly I recommend this as the safest and most direct route to that remarkable viewpoint. Contour across the moor eastward, if you locate the cross of stones laid upon the peat, then you will be precisely following in my footsteps! The view north is expansive from Laddow by Black Hill 1908' and the Holme Moss mast to Britland Edge 1717' and Withens Edge. Cross Far Black Clough and descend with the bulldozed track to a choice of fords.

37

WALK 5   BLEAKLOW HEAD

Bleaklow Head

from Crowden   8¼ miles

The name Bleaklow Head would appear to be something of a misnomer as normally the appendage 'Head' applies to some draining watercourse, by this convention the summit would be called 'Dowstone Head' or a name from one of several other equally valid contending streams. The use of 'Head' here must have a different slant, possibly referring to its situation at the end of the Bleaklow ridge standing proud when viewed from the west.

Glancing at the Tourist Map Bleaklow Head is the most natural of objectives from a Crowden base, but as the ground rises concave then convex this lofty outpost plays no part in the Longdendale scene. All the attention southward is held by the battlemented escarpment that shields the gently rising heather and peat moor. Into this gritstone wall slips the enticing cleft of Wildboar Clough (see drawing opposite) directly across the valley from Crowden, and walkers are commonly drawn to investigate its innermost secrets in the mistaken belief that it may easily be ascended. This is definitely not the case for, as with Shining Clough, the actual stream bed is very steeply stepped and demands a more than rudimentary knowledge of rock climbing techniques. All told this is the easiest line of assault to Bleaklow Head - just keep out of **that** clough!

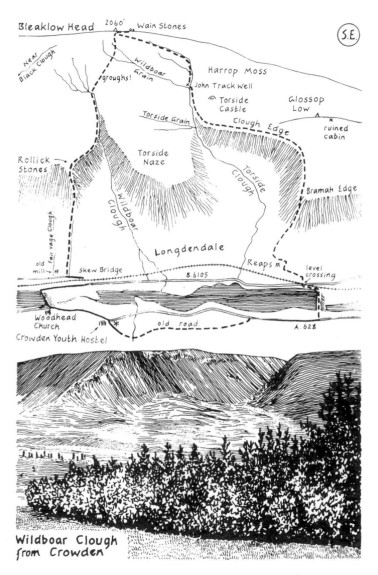

Bleaklow Head 2060' Wain Stones S.E.

Near Black Clough

groughs!

Wildboar Grain

Harrop Moss

John Track Well

Torside Castle

Glossop Low

ruined cabin

Torside Grain

Clough Edge

Rollick Stones

Torside Naze

Torside Clough

Bramah Edge

Wildboar Clough

Fair vage Clough

old mill

skew Bridge

Longdendale

B.6105

Reaps

level crossing

Woodhead Church

Crowden Youth Hostel

old road

A.628

Wildboar Clough
from Crowden

39

The walk :

Start from the new car park adjacent to the Crowden Youth Hostel and follow the road route across the valley, as in Walk 4.   From Skew Bridge follow the private road for only a short distance, diverging short of the old paper mill ascending beside the first tumbling stream, above its spring aim diagonally right for the prominent ridge.   This rises to a subsidiary top, levels, then continues up a pronounced edge to the boulders on top of Rollick Stones. An unusual feature of Rollick Stones is that broken rockwalls exist on its west facing flanks, probably the result of old quarrying activities no longer evident excepting the litter of large blocks at the base.   Follow the rim into the narrowing clough, with good views down into the cascades, a clear path running amongst the peat and heather above the true right bank well beyond the fence-end.   Where the stream takes a sharp lefthand turn strike out on a bearing for the summit of Bleaklow Head (which is not visible). Navigate with total reliance on the compass across a rather unpleasant section of degenerating groughs to join the broad and largely peat free path that has accompanied Wildboar Grain thus far heading for the summit cairn. In fact there is little deviation from the original bearing set from Wildboar Clough.   It seems odd that Torside Clough should be the recipient of a Wildboar Grain, a possible cause of confusion where hasty map reading in mist assumes that it runs into Wildboar Clough.

Bleaklow Head is no viewpoint nor is the rough pile constituting the cairn raised upon a pillow mound of raw peat a spot to recline. If your thoughts have turned upon matters of great moment like food then continue to the Wain Stones and set about your rations in comparative comfort. It is intriguing to conjecture the origin of the name Wain Stones, did a wagonway exist right up here rather an unlikely theory yet they in no way resemble a cart, so why Wain?   The two principal rocks repose in such a manner that they have attracted the title 'The Kiss', sealing a grotesque romance of true grit!

The way back to Crowden runs in common with the Pennine Way, so there is a confusion of pedestrian courses initially leading downhill from the summit. In order that ground already covered is not retraced, proceed westward, only at the beginning hindered by groughs. Whilst Bleaklow Head may be a lacklustre viewpoint, the trek down to Torside Clough is graced with a fine prospect northwards to Lad's Leap, Laddow Rocks and Black Hill from this range appearing not as a sprawling wilderness but with the deep valleys casting gentle shadows adding a new form and texture to the rolling moorland expanse.   Joining a principal tributary the route descends the heather moor steadily, arriving surely at the confluence with Wild- boar Grain, hereon flows Torside Clough. A few feet between and above the watersmeet a diligent search will reveal a tiny walled spring constructed to provide a convenient trough for pack ponies, this is John Track Well, which is a reliable source of clean fresh water.

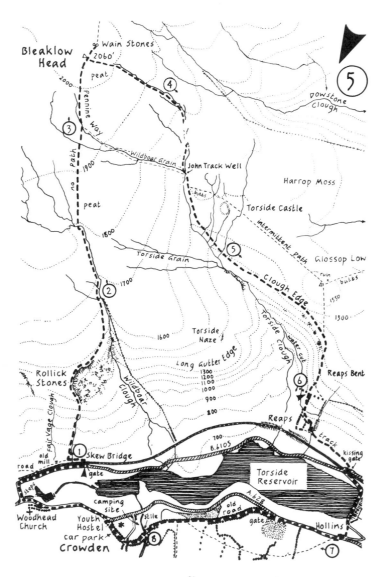

Bleaklow Head

Wain Stones
2060'

peat

pennine way

2000

③

no path

peat

1900

Wildboar Grain

John Track Well

butts

Harrop Moss

Torside Castle

intermittent path

Glossop Low

1800

④

Torside Grain

⑤

Clough Edge

ruin

butts

1550

1300

1700

②

Torside Naze

Torside Clough

Long Gutter Edge

1600

1300
1200
1100
1000
900

water cut

Reaps Bent

Rollick Stones

Wildboar Clough

⑥

800

700
B.6105

Reaps

Dowstone Clough

⑤

Fair Vage Clough

① Skew Bridge

old mill

old road

slope

camping site

gate

Torside Reservoir

A.628

old road

track

kissing gate

Woodhead Church

Youth Hostel
car park
Crowden

stile

⑧

gate

Hollins

⑦

41

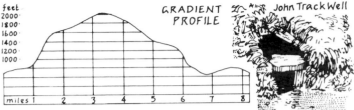

feet
2000
1800
1600
1400
1200
1000

GRADIENT PROFILE John Track Well

miles 1   2   3   4   5   6   7   8

White arrows and acorn symbols confirm the line of the Pennine Way which fords the stream, then mounts the facing bank to set course in the company of Torside Clough bound for beckoning Longdendale. A shooting path branches left serving a line of butts, and walkers who adopt this route via Glossop Low will find that the path is intermittent beyond Torside Castle. This giant mound, an artificial island of dry ground, is suggestive of some ancient signal station by its situation and simple pudding design, but whatever its original purpose its persistence as such a large monument is an indication that little has materially altered hereabouts over a long period, apart from the retreat of trees to the valleys due to the increased souring of the moor.

The main route by Clough Edge offers spacious views afforded by the broadening clough. The name Torside describes the series of rock ribs and narrow buttresses that fall away beneath the path approaching Reaps Bent. The Climbers' Guide makes mention of the unusually sharp angle of the handholds on these crags, which is in marked contrast with the rounded holds of the majority of gritstone climbing. The route descends to pass above Reaps, which should read 'reeks', as this is a particularly insalubrious maggot farm! Passing down the farm track, lined with rhododendrons, pass through the kissing gate onto the B.6105, turn right over the level-crossing, then left down the lane and across the Torside dam to mount the steps up to Hollins. Follow the pavement, right, beside the busy A.628 for a quarter-mile, branching onto the lane beyond the cottage left, this, the old highway, leads back to Crowden.

looking north

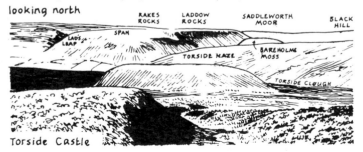

RAKES ROCKS   LADDOW ROCKS   SADDLEWORTH MOOR   BLACK HILL

SPAN

LADS LEAP

TORSIDE MAZE   BAREHOLME MOSS

TORSIDE CLOUGH

Torside Castle

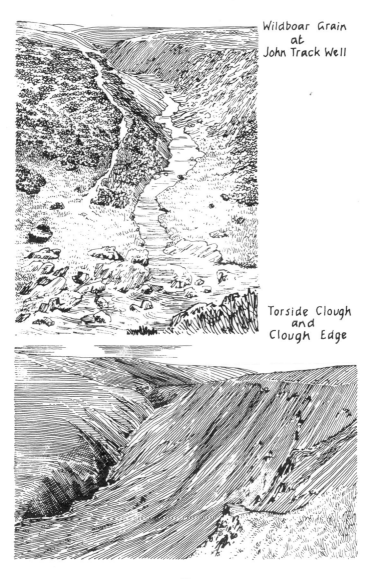

Wildboar Grain
at
John Track Well

Torside Clough
and
Clough Edge

43

WALK 6

BLEAKLOW HEAD and HIGHER SHELF STONES

from Old Glossop

8½ miles

summit of Higher Shelf Stones

LADDOW ROCKS BLACK HILL

The Glossop of today is a manifestation of cotton manufacturing which was drawn to centre on the turnpike cross-roads. Colloquially known as Howardtown, this eighteenth and nineteenth century growth left the original settlement, around the parish church, untouched, so the drift of mainstream activity rarely impinges upon Old Glossop's seclusion and olde worlde charm.

Walkers may advance into the hills from Shepley Street, a broad streamside road serving the Union Carbide factory which is situated on the site of a nineteenth century water-power textile mill and rope works with Lord Howard's saw-mill at the west end of the site.

Doctor's Gate – The walled lane that proceeds up the valley from Shepley Street is part of the Doctor's Gate trade route that for so long was thought to be of Roman origin. However, historians are now inclined to believe that it is a classic example of a late medieval packhorse 'gate' (road) constructed to link two otherwise remote valleys. Nature did not offer a low inter-connecting pass into the Woodlands valley and the Romans surveyed a route to suit their requirements and took a gentle gradient line paying little heed to the extent of swampy ground encountered and in consequence their 'road' rapidly fell from favour to be lost in the peaty morass over Moss Castle. The later expedient of a more direct route, taking the shortest crossing, saw the development of the steep Shelf Brook / Lady Clough route. Dr. Talbot may have had good reason to encourage the people from the Derwent valley to trade in Glossopdale, so he may have been instrumental in properly surfacing the pass.

44

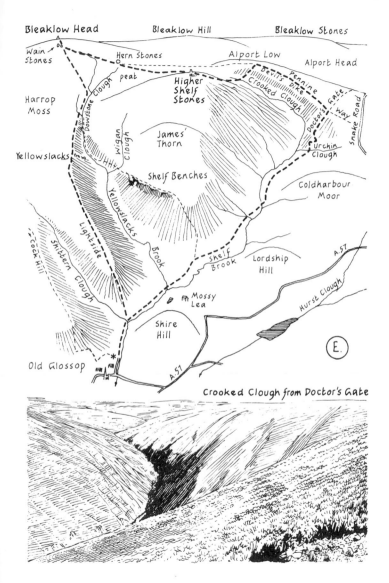

Crooked Clough from Doctor's Gate

(E.)

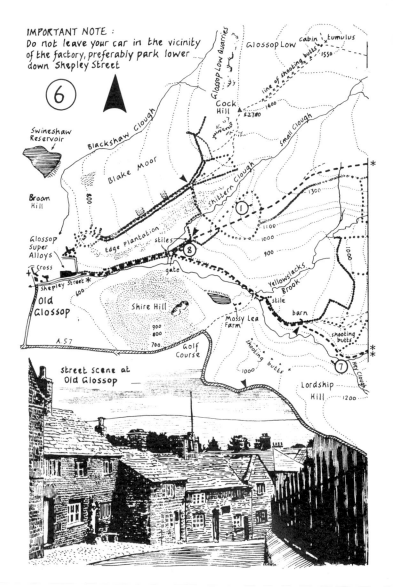

IMPORTANT NOTE :
Do not leave your car in the vicinity
of the factory, preferably park lower
down Shepley Street

⑥

Swineshaw
Reservoir

Broom
Hill

Glossop
Super
Alloys

+ cross

Shepley Street

Old
Glossop

A.57

Blackshaw Clough

Blake Moor

Edge Plantation

Shire Hill

Golf
Course

stiles

⑧

gate

900
800
700

1000

Glossop Low Quarries

Glossop Low

Cock
Hill

Shittern Clough

Yellowslacks Brook

stile

Mossy Lea
Farm

shooting butts

cabin

tumulus

1550

line of shooting butts

1400

▲ 1740

Small Clough

1300

1100

1000

900

barn

shooting
butts

⑦

Lordship
Hill

1200

Hey Clough

street scene at
Old Glossop

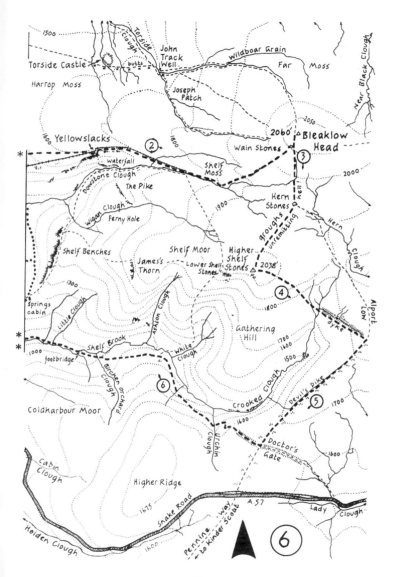

1500

Torside Clough

John Track Well

Wildboar Grain

Far Moss

Near Black Clough

Torside Castle

butts

Harrop Moss

Joseph Patch

2050

1800

Yellowslacks

②

1800

Wain Stones

2060' Bleaklow Head

③

waterfall

Shelf Moss

2000

Dowstone Clough

The Pike

Hern Stones

Wigan Clough

1900

cloughs unremitting

Ferny Hole

Hern Clough

Shelf Benches

Shelf Moor

Higher Shelf Stones

James's Thorn

Lower Shelf Stones

2038 △

Alport Low

1300

④

1800

springs cabin

Little Clough

Gathering Hill

1700
1600

Shelf Brook

Ashton Clough

1500

1000

White Clough

footbridge

Birchen or Orchard Clough

⑥

Crooked Clough

Devil's Pike

⑤

1700

Coldharbour Moor

Urchin Clough

1600

Doctor's Gate

1600

Cabin Clough

Higher Ridge

1675

Snake Road   A 57

Lady Clough

Holden Clough

1600

Pennine Way to Kinder Scout

⑥

47

There is a strong element of choice open to the walker starting his ascent of the Bleaklow massif from Old Glossop, and indeed I have plotted three routes to Bleaklow Head and the same number of options for the descent from Higher Shelf Stones. The prime and most direct approach mounts the ridge between Shittern and Dowstone Cloughs: however, a delightful rocky alternative goes by Shelf Benches into Dowstone Clough, holding most promise for the scrambler. An old quarry lane leads up to Cock Hill, this longer route giving the widest prospects.

The Walk :

Following the lane from the factory branch at the ladder stile just short of the lane gate, a fence confining the path by the wall up to an access point stile, and a well used path, thereafter, climbs the Lightside ridge. Shittern Clough (a rather surprising name for it means precisely what it suggests!) retreats from view as the walker is naturally drawn towards the Yellowslacks edge. Cross the fence, erected to keep sheep from the rocky declivity of Yellowslacks, the Ordnance Survey pinpoints a Dog Rock, whatever that may be, and uncharacteristically gives an erroneous location for the Yellowslacks crag which is close to the Dog Rock about the 1500' contour. Keeping close company with the fence into the clough take a bearing on Wain Stones: as the clough begins to lose its identity, the going gets appreciably stickier near the prominent stones and few walkers simply march past without at least kicking the peat from their boots. It is but a short step further to the actual cairn marking Bleaklow Head. Little time needing to be spent here, turnabout setting your sights on Hern Stones. Progress can be painfully slow through the badly eroded peaty morass. Hern Stones reside plumb on the watershed of England, rainwater splashing off these rocks flow with agonising sloth through the maze of grough channels eventually seeping either west into the Etherow, Goyt, Tame and Mersey for the Irish Sea or east into the Alport, Derwent, Trent and Humber for the North Sea. Once again take a compass bearing on Higher Shelf Stones, trusting in its infallibility across a further stretch of diabolical groughs, reaching the O.S. column with some relief. This is a marvellous viewpoint, quite the best on Bleaklow, indeed the Ordnance Survey by their location of a triangulation column (s.3627) seem to be of the same opinion, but it is inclined to be windy, catching the up draught from the depths of the Shelf Brook valley.

view S.S.E. from Lower Shelf Stones

ASHOP EDGE - KINDER SCOUT
course of the Pennine Way
MOSS CASTLE
A 57
course of Roman Road leading down the Wood's Cabin ridge into the suburbs of Glossop, from Ashop by way of Upper Gate Clough.

SHINING TOR
WINDGATHER ROCKS
MOUNT FAMINE
MILL HILL

CHINLEY CHURN
LEYGATEHEAD MOOR
COLDHARBOUR MOOR

URCHIN CLOUGH
Doctor's Gate
Shelf Brook Valley ↓

Walkers may leave this distinct summit by either Lower Shelf Stones with the option of a steep descent into White Clough or more gently by Jame's Thorn to Shelf Benches and the derelict Springs Cabin (beware of the waterfalls if Ashton Clough is tried). Or descend the easy slopes south-eastwards to the head of Crooked Clough (I cannot comment on its suitability having not explored this obvious watercourse), and thence up the prominent dyke onto Alport Low.

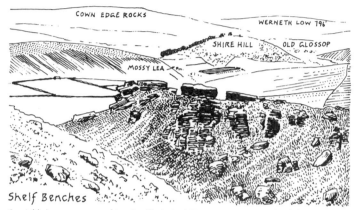

COWN EDGE ROCKS

WERNETH LOW 796'

SHIRE HILL   OLD GLOSSOP

MOSSY LEA Fm.

Shelf Benches

Go right to accompany the Devil's Dyke (the name recognises that this was a boundary trench its original purpose being sufficiently obscure, possibly Dark Age, for its function not to have survived as a folk memory, the widely practised custom being to credit unnatural features to the devil). The spongy ridge is forsaken at Doctor's Gate (the causeway was named after Dr. John Talbot, who was vicar at Glossop between 1494-1550), at last a dryshod track putting walkers on course back to the valley. The way zig-zags through Urchin Clough, a most intriguing name possibly compounded from 'chin' which appears in Chinley and means a steep valley and 'ur' which is similarly Old Norse and means a kind of ox. The scenery is most impressive, reminiscent of some wild Highland glen, the romantic seclusion   only gently broken in the latter stages as the roughly surfaced track returns to the lane into Old Glossop.

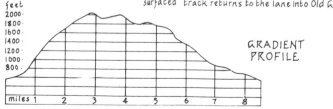

feet
2000
1800
1600
1400
1200
1000
800

GRADIENT
PROFILE

miles 1   2   3   4   5   6   7   8

49

Dowstone Clough from Yellowslacks

Rock climbing on Yellowslacks blossomed after the last war but in the early 1960's the farmers at Mossy Lea were so incensed by the popularity of this fine bastion that they brought in contractors to blast the crag into oblivion, on the dubious pretext of purging the crag of loose rock which they claimed was a danger to grazing sheep!

Mercifully, despite two separate attempts they were unable to completely emasculate it. The Peak Planning Board managed to resolve the problem through the provisions of access agreements worked out with the National Farmers Union, thereby ensuring that farmers were compensated for potential damage or interference. Climbing here was now permitted provided, of course, that the bye-laws posted at all access points were strictly followed.

Doctor's Gate

Dowstone Clough

Wain Stones
"The Kiss"

WALK 7 — ALPORT DALE and the WOODLANDS VALLEY

from Alport Bridge

12 miles

Bleaklow may have an austere reputation but the determined explorer who tracks up Alport Dale will have an advantage over the Pennine Way or Derwent Watershed sojourners, for this is Bleaklow's prized possession.   A sequestered hamlet, an 'awe-inspiring' 'crag-shattered' landslip and a deep sinuous valley course leading to a wild secluded bowl in the hills at Grains-in-the-water. This isolation is heightened by the fact that from the hamlet right up to Glethering Clough there is no access in the valley. Walkers are reminded that this restriction must be respected; neither, it must be stressed, may walkers venture into Ouzelden Clough (blackbird valley) or the Westend valley — help preserve what few sanctuaries remain.

The Woodlands valley comes in sharp contrast to the lonely confines of the Alport Dale, though no less pleasant in its own way. Yes, there are trees — thousands of them, marching down Lady Clough - alien conifers, but the scene would be barren without them, so much original woodland having gone. The valley itself is on a grander scale, below Lady Clough, flanked by the imposing north-west buttresses of Kinder Scout. The walk finds a peaceful refuge in the company of the ancient Roman trackway well above the hubbub of the Snake road.   This has long been a settled valley and until the 7th Duke of Devonshire instigated the Turnpike coaching road (the Snake Road is named after the Snake Inn, which in turn takes its name from the Cavendish, Dukes of Devonshire, family crest), linking Sheffield with Glossop, the valley must have been little affected by the upheavals of the outside world. The effect of bringing a flood of trans-Pennine traffic was nowhere near as mortal a blow as the impounding of the Ashop by the Ladybower Dam. It was from this vale that the Woodland Whiteface sheep originated, a hardy mountain breed noted for the high quality of its wool (the result of cross-breeding with the Spanish Merino introduced at the time of King George III, it is now rare).

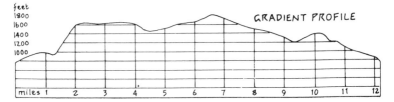

GRADIENT PROFILE

feet 1800 1600 1400 1200 1000

miles 1 2 3 4 5 6 7 8 9 10 11 12

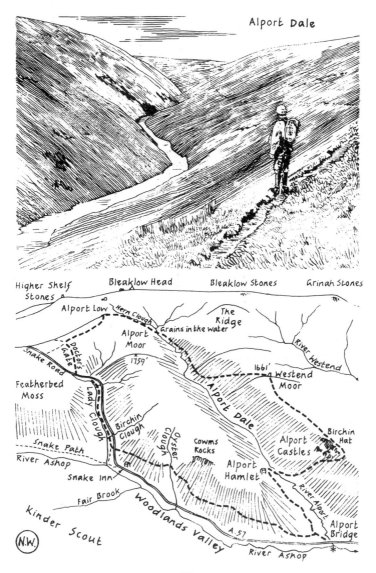

Alport Dale

Higher Shelf Stones   Bleaklow Head   Bleaklow Stones   Grinah Stones

Alport Low   Hern Clough   The Ridge
Grains in the water
Alport Moor
Snake Road   Doctor's Gate
Feather bed Moss   Lady Clough   1759'
River Westend
1661'   Westend Moor
Alport Dale
Snake Path   Birchin Clough
River Ashop   Oyster Clough   Cowms Rocks
Birchin Hat
Alport Castles
Snake Inn
Fair Brook   Alport Hamlet
River Alport
Woodlands Valley
Kinder Scout   A.57   Alport Bridge
River Ashop

(N.W.)

53

Alport Hamlet

Looking up Alport Dale from Alport Castles

THE TOWER   HIGHER SHELF   BLEAKLOW
              STONES   HEAD

The Walk:

The walk has two potential starting points. Birchin Clough, where the Snake road once kinked, has been made into a useful car park and has greater parking scope than Alport Bridge, which I have chosen. Alport Bridge (an unauthorised car park) is the natural springboard for this excursion.   Follow the track to the Alport Hamlet (no longer even a farm residence), which is the venue of an annual 'Love Feast' on the first Sunday in July. This tradition stems from the time when this remote community was the perfect retreat for Nonconformist services, when such gatherings were made illegal by Charles II in 1662.   The track continues through the buildings and proceeds round with the wall to a ford. Fortunately there is a substantial footbridge at hand.

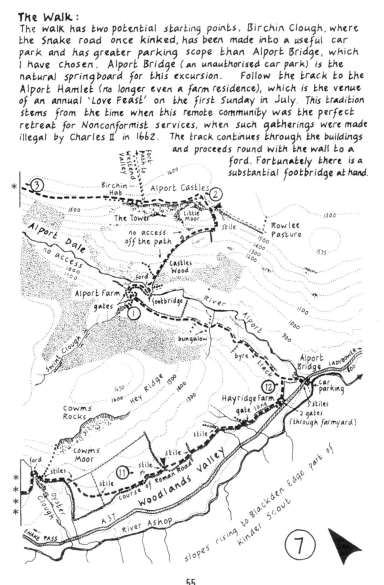

Seal Edge   Fairbrook Naze   Ashop Edge

Swint Clough

The Tower, Alport Castles

Alport Dale from above Glethering Clough

Upper confines of Hern Clough

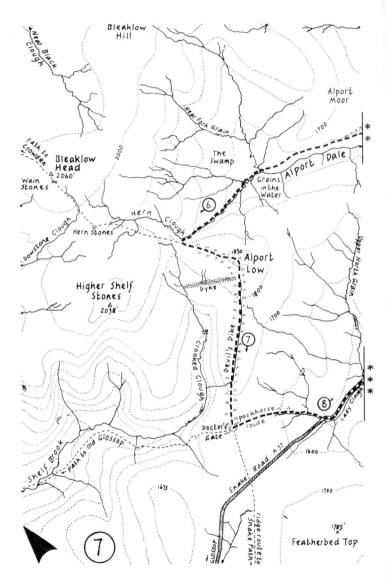

Near Black Clough

Bleaklow Hill

Alport Moor

New Fork Grain

1700

Path to Crowden

Bleaklow Head
△ 2060'

Wain Stones

2000

The Swamp

Alport Dale

Grains in the Water

Dowstone Clough

Hern Clough

Hern Stones

⑥

Upper North Grain

1850

Alport Low

Dyke

1800

Higher Shelf Stones
△ 2038'

1700

⑦

Crooked Clough

Devil's Dike

Shelf Brook

Path to Old Glossop

Doctor's Gate

packhorse route

⑧

Lady Clough

Snake Road A57

1600

1675

1700

Glossop

ridge route to Snake Path

1785'
×
Featherbed Top

◀

⑦

58

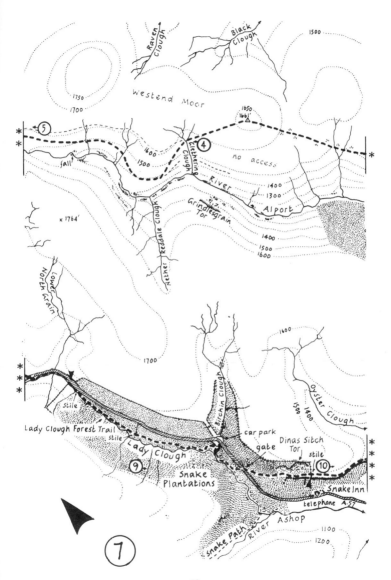

Raven Clough

Black Clough

1500

Westend Moor

1750
1700

⑤
✱
✱

fall

1500
1600

Eelbeark Clough

④

1650
1661'
△

no access

River Alport

1400
1300

✱

x 1764'

Nether Reddale Clough

Grindlesgrain Tor

1400
1500
1600

Lower North Grain

1700

1600

Birchin Clough

Oyster Clough

1500
1400

✱
✱
✱

stile

Lady Clough Forest Trail

stile

Lady Clough

⑨

Snake Plantations

car park

gate

Dinas Sitch Tor

stile

⑩

✱
✱
✱
✱

Snake Inn

telephone A57

Snake Path

River Ashop

1100
1200

⑦

59

From the footbridge, a clear and frequently used footpath progresses uphill beside the fence, Alport Castles dominates the ascent. Do not leave the path to explore the environs of the cliffs, rather continue to the wall stile. Now follow the wall up to the access point then up to the skyline, following the edge left to admire the profound declivity. Alport Castles is the result of an enormous landslip, The Tower stands proud, severed by a giant upheaval, far below its original resting place. At one time this must have been a lateral cleft much as exists today at Lud's Church (see Walk 22), and has eroded down to a humbled shadow of its former grandeur. The footpath quits the ridge from Birchin Hat down into the foot of Westend valley. However, our journey heads along the edge path with the Alport valley to the lonely O.S. column on Westend Moor.

STANAGE END   HIGH NEB   STANAGE EDGE   BAMFORD EDGE   TOTLEY MOOR   BIRCHINLEE PASTURE   WIN HILL PIKE   BIRCHIN HAT

DERWENT EDGE

View S.E. from Westend Moor   intermittent path from Alport Castles

Absorb the moorland panorama from this spot, for the long skylines of Bleaklow, Howden Moor, Derwent Edge and Kinder Scout almost completely shuts off the outside world. The one breach is south-east where the flanking edges above the Derwent stretch away, Totley Moor being some twenty miles distant and Eyam Moor is but a little less.

Whilst you may retain the broad and frequently wet ridge to embrace the peaty wastes of Bleaklow proper, my preferred route diverts down to the head of Glethering Clough (which means sheep gathering) and slants down to join the contouring trod that leads up this exquisite winding dale, quite the best of Bleaklow's watercourses. A path also follows the edge but does not match the lower path for intimacy and sheer pleasurable walking. The valley opens out approaching Grains-in-the-water, which implies a boggy watersmeet, but despite the presence on maps of The Swamp, the ground is not especially wet. Ford the stream following Hern Clough, west, up its ravine, emerging onto the peaty watershed go left, now in the company of the Pennine Way, over Alport Low marked by a stake.

BLEAKLOW STONES   GRINAH STONES

Alport Low is the highest point on this
excursion but by no stretch of the
imagination is it a memorable
viewpoint, nor could the soggy and
gently declining ridge to Doctor's
Gate be pronounced a joyous
romp. Yet the Devil's Dike leads
unerringly to the paved causeway and departs from the ridge
more pleasantly.

There is some merit in glancing over
the shoulder of Alport Low into
Upper North Grain: if nothing else
it will take away some enforced
roadwalking. The Snake Road is
followed the short distance down
to Upper North Grain, then the route
is at liberty to slip down the bank to
accompany Lady Clough, beyond the
recently erected mini-clapper bridge
over Lower North Grain, to enter the

Seal Stones from Oyster Clough

Lady Clough Forest Trail, which runs a devious course through the conifers.

Below Birchin Clough branch left up the forestry track to the padlocked
gate, cross the A.57 to join the footpath slanting up through the conifers,
occasionally hindered by fallen trees, pass under the shattered Dinas Sitch
Tor to a stile into open pasture. Follow the well defined path by the wall
and fence into Oyster Clough. Surely this is no reference to shellfish: may it
mean a secretive place? Hereon an obvious path passes, by a series of
stile, through pastureland to the sunken lane to and behind Hayridge Farm.

WALK 8   BLEAKLOW STONES

from King's Tree
or Fairholmes car park

10¾ miles
(if you miss the bus - 20 miles !!)

To gain the fullest value from an expedition to Bleaklow Stones
it is advisable to bear in mind that they are remotely sited,
and they are made all the more enisled when the road by Derwent
and Howden Reservoirs is debarred from vehicular access.   This
restriction operates over weekends and Bank Holidays from
Good Friday till the end of October, adding just under ten miles
of hard tarmac to this walk - a minibus service exists at such
times, but do check the timetable in the information centre at
Fairholme, if you intend to avoid the long walk back.

Bleaklow Stones make a fine vantage and if your visit coincides
with good visibility then it will reward the fortunate visitor
with extensive prospects to north and south.   However, this
happy state of affairs is not common, and at times of low
cloud or deteriorating visibility it would be prudent to either
content yourself with Barrow and Grinah Stones or reduce
your circuit even more by ascending Lower Small Clough. I can
heartily recommend this latter action, for, by slipping over Ronksley
Moor into Linch Clough, much of the wilderness aspect of these
lonely moors is revealed without over exposing the walker to
too much vigorous and trackless going.

Walkers who delight in tracing rivers to their source will enjoy
the upper Derwent (formerly Ronksley River) until they near
Swains Greave. If, having also looked up the place-name
derivation and discovering that Swains Greave translates to
'pig's grove', you feel tempted to seek out this sequestered copse,
I must hasten to inform you that the name would be more appropriate
if it read 'Swains Grave', as the peat rises in giant hags and
soggy channels. It is possible that the place-name was transferred
up the valley for no tree has grown in this inhospitable spot for
literally thousands of years - comfortably pre-dating the place-name.

The name Barrow Stones should not be construed as a reference to
some obscure burial mound raised symbolically upon this prominent
coign.   If that were the case then they would be distinguished by
the only word common in Peakland for such a feature 'Low.' The rocks
were named from the watercourse below, being recorded in 1627 as
'Barow Clough stone'. I believe the word 'barow' in this connection
is associated with trees, birch or alder.

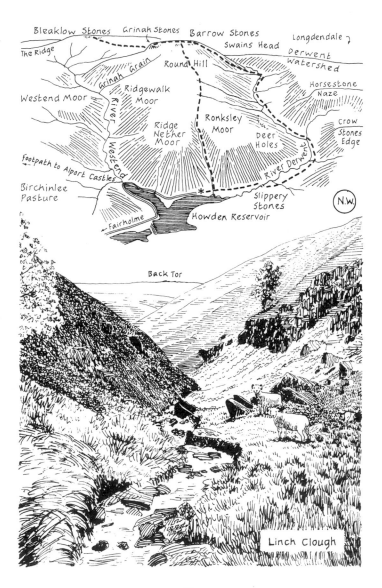

Bleaklow Stones   Grinah Stones   Barrow Stones   Longdendale
The Ridge   Swains Head   Derwent
                          Round Hill   Watershed
Grinah Grain   Horsestone
Ridgewalk   Naze
Westend Moor   Moor   Crow
                    Ridge   Ronksley   Stones
                    Nether   Moor   Edge
                    Moor   Deer
                                            Holes
Footpath to Alport Castles   River Derwent
Birchinlee   *   Slippery
Pasture   Stones   N.W.
              Fairholme   Howden Reservoir

Back Tor

Linch Clough

63

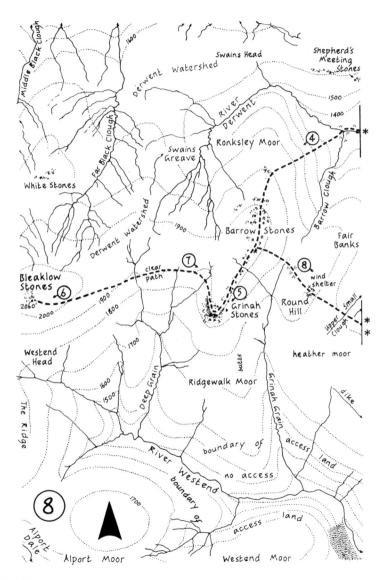

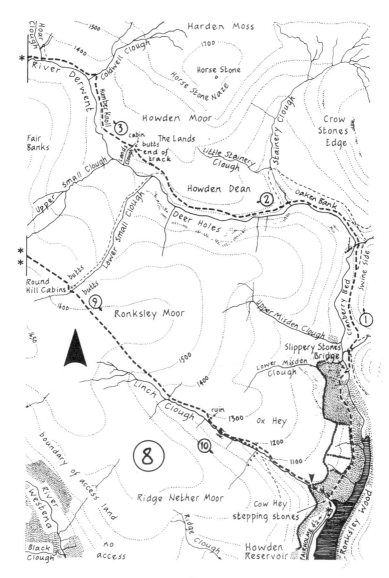

The Walk:

The King's Tree stands at the roadend from where there is an open prospect across the Howden Reservoir (see walk 9). Your car may be parked here only if you arrive either on a weekday in summer or during the winter months.

The track heads off from the barrier, crosses the stepping stones where Linch Clough debouches into the peat darkened waters of the Reservoir. The track proceeds through the conifers, planted into the old walled enclosures of pre-reservoir days, to cross Slippery Stones Bridge. A plaque on it reads 'This 17th.C. packhorse bridge whose original site at Derwent was submerged was re-erected in 1959 by public subscription as a memorial to John Derry 1854-1937 who inspired in others his love for the Derbyshire and Yorkshire Hills'. For many visitors, who perforce had to commence their foray at Fairholme, this attractive spot marks the limit of their walk, which therefore becomes a circuit of the two upper reservoirs - probably the gentlest and most rewarding of walks (cycle rides) that the High Peak can offer the non-committed walker.

Go left with the Land Rover track crossing the Fred Heardman Memorial Footbridge (Fred was a greatly respected rambler and publican, owning two inns in Edale, the Nag's Head and the Church). Branch left from the Cut (Cart) Gate track going forward in the company of an obvious track. The Derwent Valley shies westward from Broadhead Clough so leading the walker into a remote region where rises this great river. The valley slopes are bestrewn with stunted and gnarled trees and stumps, hence Oaken Bank. Deer Holes (like Deer Knowl over on the Etherow flank of Bleaklow) suggests that at one time the moors supported wild herds of deer, long departed from the scene.

Slippery Stones Bridge

Upper Derwentdale featuring Ronksley River and Horsestone Naze

BLACK HILL   HOLME MOSS

HEYDEN HEAD

HEYDEN BROOK

SWAIN'S HEAD

Barrow Stones

path to and from
Bleaklow Stones

Grinah Stones looking to Bleaklow Stones

LOOKING NORTH

BLACK HILL 5½ miles · HAWORTH MOOR 26 miles · ILKLEY MOOR 31 miles

TOOLEYSHAW MOSS · HEYDEN HEAD · HOLME MOSS · BRITLAND EDGE HILL

BLEAKLOW MEADOWS

LOOKING EAST

MARGERY HILL · GRINAH STONES · HIGH STONES · ROW TOP · ABBEY BROOK

RONKSLEY MOOR

Two views from the summit rocks of Bleaklow Stones

The scenery becomes progressively more barren rising gently to Lands Clough where the track ceases - servicing the shooting butts on The Lands, hence the snug corrugated cabin, and the butts higher up Lower Small Clough. Henceforward an indefinite path leads on over Humber Knoll in close company with the Ronksley stream. Ronksley was a farm submerged beneath Howden Reservoir and took its name from an unrecorded personal name from Old English 'ranc' meaning proud or insolent, therefore the place meant 'Ranc's clearing' - no doubt all the high ground between Linch Clough and the Derwent had belonged to this holding.

Fording Coldwell and Hoar Cloughs the preferred route crosses the infant Derwent, near its confluence with Barrow Clough, and climbs the trackless moor onto Barrow Stones. Progress from Humber Knoll to these outcrops is as strenuous as at any stage of this walk, and the comparatively easy parade to Grinah Stones will be appreciated, not least for the view, notably the eastward prospect to Howden and Derwent Edges.

Grinah simply means 'grains wells' and the large fractured and weathered outcrop of gritstone harbours a diversity of hardy plants and wild life, walkers too find their shelter of value - a rare commodity on Bleaklow's notoriously inhospitable plateau.

A well used trod works round the headwaters of Deep Grain up to Bleaklow Stones. Fortunately, the immediate surroundings of the Stones is not over-encumbered with peat so the rocks stand starkly proud, defiant against the torments and ravages of a hostile climate of wind, frost and rain. The Stones are worth inspecting, even if visibility denies the full extensive view, there are several intriguing formations the impressive three-pronged Trident and the Anvil Stone (see illustration on previous page), and numerous etchings, the graffiti of countless transitory idle moments.

Return to Grinah Stones. However, if your destination is Fairholme, proceed on a southerly course round Westend Head and over Alport Moor to Alport Castles, continue over Rowlee Pasture descending to the track by Bellhagg Barn reaching the car park on the permissive path descending by Lockerbrook. The illustrated route backtracks to the large outcrop just short of Barrow Stones before diverting down the slope on a south-easterly arc to the prominent cairn cum wind shelter on Round Hill. Take a bearing now on the cabins in Lower Small Clough, they are not marked on Ordnance Survey maps but can be located at Grid Ref. 146957.

Round Hill Cabins, as they are known, can offer welcome temporary accommodation for a large party, though walkers are on honour not to abuse the free access, if they had to be locked though some wanton act, a vital emergency shelter would be lost.

Maintain your course with only a tiny modification of bearing to enter Linch Clough, the name means 'the ridge ravine' and certainly it cuts a deep course into Ronksley Moor, narrowing from 1300', and allowing little scope for a path. The most practical line keeps to the left bank, joining a grass track where it fords at 1100', passing down through the trees to the stepping stones and the King's Tree.

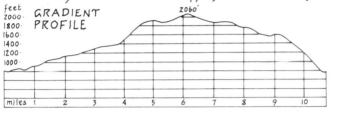

GRADIENT PROFILE

2060'

CROW STONES EDGE

Round Hill Cabins

Chapter Three

The eastern edges have been the popular haunt of Sheffield ramblers for many decades and the spacious prospects are well appreciated by devotees who, with good reason, greatly value the solitude and wild beauty they offer.   The Howden Moors from Swains Head to Dove-stone Tor to the watershed belong to the National Trust, which means that it is not strictly access land. The Trust does not close its moors for grouse shooting nor scotch access; nonetheless, it expects the same high standards of conduct from walkers as is required where open country access has been negotiated. Running north and east of the Trust's land are large tracts of grouse moor traversed by few rights of way.

The Stanage Edge walk effectively forges a link between the wild craggy exposures of Derwent Edge and the gentle pastoral land-scapes of Low Peak. Win Hill Pike is a staunch individualist, its unusual summit exuding an exuberance only rivalled by Back Tor.

Crow Stones Edge

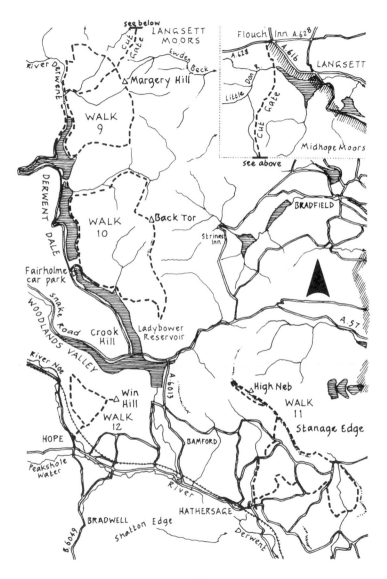

see below
LANGSETT
MOORS

River Derwent

Ewden Beck

Margery Hill

WALK
9

Flouch Inn A.628

A.628   A.616   LANGSETT

Little Don R.

Cut Gate

Midhope Moors

see above

DERWENT DALE

WALK
10

Back Tor

Strines
Inn

BRADFIELD

Fairholme
car park

Snake Road

WOODLANDS VALLEY

Crook
Hill

Ladybower
Reservoir

A.57

River Noe

A.6013

Win
Hill

WALK
12

High Neb

WALK
11

Stanage Edge

HOPE

BAMFORD

Peakshole
Water

River

BRADWELL   Shatton Edge

HATHERSAGE

Derwent

B.6049

WALK 9   HOWDEN EDGE

from the King's Tree
or Fairholmes car park

8¾ miles

Crow Stones

As a natural accompaniment to this rather delightful moorland
excursion embracing the Howden Edge, I have included a description of the Cut Gate track, advancing from the Flouch Inn. This
age old pedestrian thoroughfare must have served the remote
upper Derwent Dale for as long as settlements have existed there
and it still provides a fine approach to the delights of these
secluded eastern moors and dales.

The modern byway that winds by the western shores of the three
Derwent reservoirs comes to a halt at the King's Tree, from here
the walker may venture into an untrammelled landscape of wild hills.
Whilst one can acknowledge the necessity of damming and storing
huge reserves of water one cannot help ruing the passing of the
living soul of a remote community. Little remains to record the lives
of these hardy folk, except the higher enclosure walls and a thin
spread of place-name references.

The little frequented moors and cloughs that flank the Cut Gate track
are well worth exploring, my curiosity drew me to gain the acquaintance
of the Horse Stone above Stainery Clough, the Bull Stones and Wilfrey's
Neild but for some strange reason it was the Crow Stones that
held the greatest fascination, both as a viewpoint and for their
fantastic elemental sculpting. Connoisseurs of the north-eastern
sector of Peakland, and there are a good many who regularly tramp
along these lonely edges by choice, make Crow Stones Edge a
special objective. Their position above the Derwent Valley just where
it takes a decisive sweep southward makes this a viewpoint par excell-
ence of the eastern shoulders of Bleaklow rising in stark outline above
Ronksley Moor, flanked by Horsestone Naze to the right. To the
left, that long southerly strike of the Derwent, carries the eye
away to Abbey Bank and Derwent Edge, with Margery Hill and
High Stones figuring large more immediately at hand, both of
which are embraced on this expedition along Howden Edge.

74

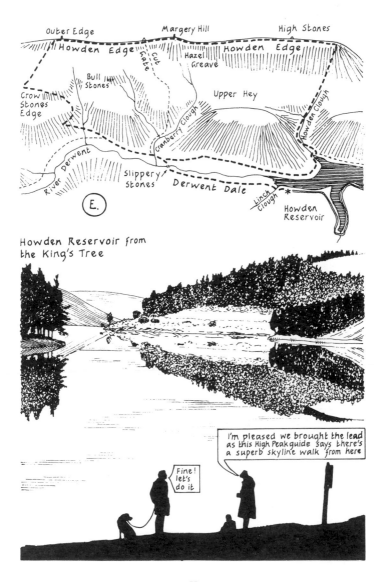

Outer Edge — Margery Hill — High Stones

Howden Edge — Howden Edge

Hazel Greave

Bull Stones — Cut Gate

Crow Stones Edge

Upper Hey

Howden Clough

Cranberry Clough

River Derwent

Slippery Stones — Derwent Dale

Linch Clough

Howden Reservoir

E.

Howden Reservoir from the King's Tree

I'm pleased we brought the lead as this High Peak guide says there's a superb skyline walk from here

Fine! let's do it

The Walk:

This fine expedition along the west facing edges of Howden Moor, starts as per WALK 8. However, beyond Cranberry Bed take the rising path from the Land-Rover track leading up into Broadhead Clough. Ford the stream, then rise more steeply on an engineered path that crosses Oaken Bank. Watch for the path doubling back at the highest point, this level path leads past two ruined cabins (offering no shelter), to a walled spring. Grandly titled, Lord Edward Howard's Spring, this occasional fresh water supply must have been appreciated back in the days of exclusive rights just as it is today with the greater liberties afforded under the National Trust's custodianship. Climb off the shooter's path, at this point, to take a diagonal course up the rough and steepening scarp to the skyline, where pick up the thinnest of sheep trods along Crow Stones Edge.

The Crow Stones would be an admirable place to halt awhile, to clamber or shelter from the not infrequent stiff breeze emanating from the broad exposed flanks of Bleaklow. The more familiar Salt Cellar on Derwent Edge has a rival here and from one angle a crudely mimicked Dancing Bear of Brimham sits up (see beginning of chapter).

The way across to Outer Edge is likely to be wet and two significant groughs hamper progress further. Beyond the shattered edge locate the watershed path, regularly confirmed by stakes (which come into real play when a blanket mist takes away the few landmarks). The O.S. column stands too far back from Outer Edge to lend it any virtue as a viewpoint so there is little cause to break one's stride to inspect it. The soggy path to Margery Hill is largely devoid of gradient, and to be frank, interest either. A more interesting variation is to veer from the column on Outer Edge across the pathless moor above Broadhead to the Bull Stones, the haunt of blue hares and foxes. Contour then to the signpost above the steep rise of Little Cut, proceeding along the old beater's trod to Wilfrey Neild, a better vantage than is obtained from the O.S. column on nearby Margery Hill. The ridge path merges with the edge path mounting onto High Stones. The views are enhanced both by the steep declivity and the rocky outcrops along this prominent escarpment, the route declines, with the edge to Row Top, though walkers may prefer to keep with the high ground beyond the Wet Stones to delve into the headwaters of Abbey Brook. Row Top is a good viewpoint into the deep trough of Abbey Brook. The O.S. ascribe Howden Dean to this valley, which seems an odd duplication (to match the Bull Cloughs of Cut Gate) for Howden meant 'deep valley' and Dean also meant 'valley'.

At the cross wall go right with the broken wall down into Howden Clough. Picking up a thin path pass the rainfall measurement pond and the forestry onto the reservoir track, going right to Slippery Stones or left for Fairholme.

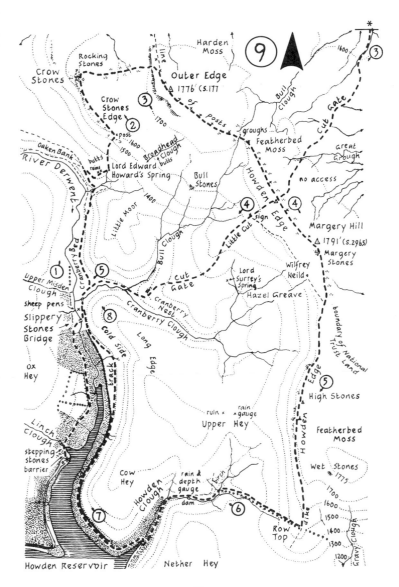

Harden Moss

⑨

*

Rocking Stones

Crow Stones

Outer Edge
△ 1776' (S.177

line of posts

1600

③

Bull Clough

Cut Gate

Crow Stones Edge
②

③
post
1700
1600
1500

Broadhead Clough

Lord Edward
Howard's Spring

butts ruins

Lord Edward butts

Bull Stones

groughs

Featherbed Moss

great Clough

no access

Oaken Bank

River Derwent

Little Moor

1400

Bull Clough

Cranberry Bed

④ sign
④

Howden Edge

Margery Hill
△ 1791' (S.2965)

Margery Stones

①
Upper Misden Clough

sheep pens

Slippery Stones Bridge

ox Hey

⑤

Cut Gate

1700

Little Cut Gate

Cranberry Nest

Lord Surrey's Spring

Wilfrey Neild

Hazel Greave

boundary of National Trust Land

⑧

Cranberry Clough

Long Edge

Cold Side

track

⑤
High Stones

Featherbed Moss

Linch Clough

stepping stones barrier

Cow Hey

Upper Hey

ruin × rain × gauge

Howden Clough

rain & depth gauge

birch

dam

⑥

Wet Stones
1775

1700
1600
1500
1400
1300
1200

Gravy Clough

⑦

Row Top

Howden Reservoir

Nether Hey

77

High Stones from Margery Stones (above)
Margery Hill from High Stones (below)

(top) Cut Gate
(middle) Wilfrey Neild
(bottom) Derwent Dale
from Crow Stones Edge

HORSESTONE NAZE   CROW STONES EDGE   OUTER EDGE

WIN HILL   LOSE HILL   CROOKSTONE KNOLL

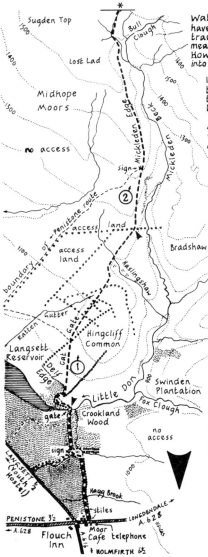

Walkers from South Yorkshire have long used the Cut Gate track, originally 'Cart Gate', as a means to advance onto the Howden Moors and Bleaklow and into the Derwent's fair dale.

It served as a trade route, linking the market at Penistone with the vast sheepwalks of the Derwent and Woodlands valleys.

A Youth Hostel at Langsett ensures this old way retains a steady flow of Wayfarers, as too the 'Cal-Der-Went Walk' which stretches from Horbury Bridge near Wakefield slipping over Cut Gate to Ladybower.

The Flouch Inn is the most common starting point, situated at an important crossroads giving good access from Manchester, Sheffield, Barnsley and Huddersfield.

A popular path circuits Langsett Reservoir offering pleasant views, but it does not run close to the water, please heed.

Over Hingcliff Common (open access) the track strangely bears the name Cat Gate. The route is extremely well marked (some may say eroded to a scar in places) and enjoys improving views as Mickleden Edge is climbed. Shades of Great Langdale, the stream below is called, rather curiously, Mickleden Beck, which means 'the large valley'.

The character of the walk alters from above Bull Clough for the path serpentines through the peat moor dodging large groughs as it goes. The occasional cairn confirming the obvious path, to eventually emerge at 1700' into the vastness of High Peakland upon Howden Edge.

The way descends purposefully into the valley, all the while open to excellent views notably of Bull Clough with Bull Stones prominent at its head.

80

The Flouch Inn

Little Don River

Mickleden Edge

WALK 10   DERWENT EDGE

from Fairholme car park

10¼ miles

The recently created car parking facility at Fairholme makes a good base for an expedition onto Derwent Edge. Experience has shown that only a tiny proportion of the inevitably large number of visitors will venture far from the security of the valley. So whilst the immediate surrounds of Fairholme may be a throng with activity during fine weekends those that do journey into the hills will find a lingering peace and be richly rewarded for their effort.

Abbey Brook cuts a deep and exciting divide between the wild and expansive Howden Moors and the more popular Derwent Edge. The advance up the valley holds high promise for unlike the common pattern of the lesser cloughs upon these moors, Howden Dean does not quickly merge into barren moorland but sustains a mystique drawing the walker into the heart of the hills. The trackless moor from Sheepfold Clough to Lost Lad is the only blemish to this trip, for with viewpoints and gritstone tors aplenty the walker has every reason to dawdle and delight in each new step down the long ridge to Whinstone Lee Tor.

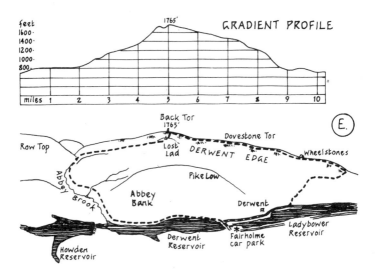

summit of Back Tor

summit of Lost Lad

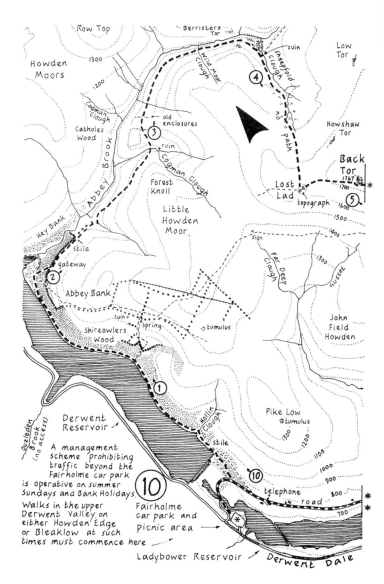

Row Top

Berristers Tor

ruin

Low Tor

Howden Moors

1300

Wild Moor

Sheepfold Clough

④

no path

Howshaw Tor

1200

Cogman Clough

old enclosures

③

Catholes Wood

ruin

Abbey Brook

Cogman Clough

Back Tor
1761
1700

Lost Lad

topograph

⑤

1600

Forest Knoll

Little Howden Moor

1500

Hey Bank

1400

sign

Fair Deep Clough

1300

Gusset

stile

gateway

②

Abbey Bank

tumulus

John Field Howden

ruin

spring

Shireowlers Wood

Derwent Reservoir

①

Hollin Clough

Pike Low
tumulus

1300

1200

1100

Ouzleden Brook (no access)

stile

1000

900

A management scheme prohibiting traffic beyond the Fairholme car park is operative on summer Sundays and Bank Holidays.

⑩

telephone

road

800

Walks in the upper Derwent Valley on either Howden Edge or Bleaklow at such times must commence here

Fairholme car park and picnic area

100

Ladybower Reservoir

Derwent Dale

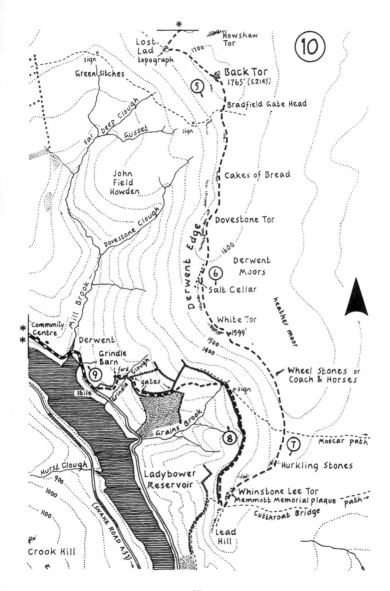

The Walk:

From the car park join the road to Derwent branching left immediately following the curve beneath the Derwent dam. A path climbs up through the conifers to join the reservoir track next to the dam wall. The track permits fine open prospects across the Derwent reservoir to the conifer plantations that clothe the lower moorland slopes and notably into secretive Ouzelden Clough.

Walkers seeking a more direct ascent to Back Tor can branch up through Shireowlers Wood (boundary alders - Yorkshire/Derbyshire). This soon reaches a gate giving entry to the upper pastures, the overgrown track zig-zags and is lost approaching the spring, but just above this is the clearly marked Abbey Brook path. Follow the path to Bradfield Gate Head then branch left to Back Tor summit.

The principal route continues along the reservoir track towards the Howden dam, diverging right just before Abbey Brook bridge. In spring this spot is bedecked with daffodils, a garden gone wild beside the foundations of a house. A Land-Rover track leads to a gateway then beside the forestry wall to a stile. The track is retained by Cogman Clough, this name may be linked to the Old Norse 'kuggr' which meant a merchant ship and infer a particular kind of monastic tradesman - see Cogger's Lane at Hathersage.

Row Top from Abbey Brook

Berristers Tor

Two views of Abbey Brook

The track becomes quite indistinct across an area of fine turf where low balks are suggestive of former cultivation. The valley narrows, the track climbs above the confluence, here a geological fault has fashioned an unusual rift, the north flowing Sheepfold Clough stream having cut a ravine separate from the fault. The old path continues becoming a bridleway at the watershed, an odd switch, on course for Bradfield and the Don Valley.

The illustrated route, however, goes right with Sheepfold Clough (no fold only the foundations of a shooting cabin) which opens out onto a spongy moor. Any semblance of a path is soon lost and whilst walkers may be attracted towards Howshaw Tor, it is far better to aim for Lost Lad, note the old drainage channels on the ridge north of Lost Lad. A large cairn surmounts this prominent outpost of the Derwent Edge and its virtues as a viewpoint are confirmed by the location of a topogragh, erected by the famous Sheffield Clarion Ramblers in memory of W.H.Baxby. The panoramic plate gives a useful outline of hill features on display, though its curvature unfortunately brings some distortion, which is a pity. Now follow the broad path that crosses the hill, going eastward to Back Tor. The triangulation column is most delightfully placed high upon the summit rocks, necessitating mild scrambling tactics to reach it. Standing on top of this defiant outcrop one is aware of the superb panorama. This is certainly one of the best tops in High Peak both as a viewpoint and as a spectacle of sheer naked rock. A touching piece of romance is etched into the rocks just below the summit recording – 'Mary and Jack engaged here March 5 1933'. The numerous phases of the Great Ice Age carved out the deep valleys like the Derwent, but they can never have entirely covered the moorland as the rock tors that stand proud of the present surface level testify. These remained, hard against the elements, their erosion has been a slow process, contemporary strata being wiped out, possibly by ice, with a totality that makes the remaining tors look like misplaced megaliths.

A laterally eroded path begins the steady descent of Derwent Edge: it tends to keep east of the rocky edge thus missing the more intimate features that characterise this ridge. Crossing Bradfield Gate (a footpath referred to earlier), the route passes the Cakes of Bread and Dovestone Tor. The often photographed Salt Cellar stands aside of the path commanding a fine prospect both abroad and down upon the site of the lost village of Derwent, submerged when the Ladybower dam was constructed just prior to the last war. Beyond White Tor the Wheel Stones attract attention, in dark silhouette simulating the wild dashing motion of a coach and horses fleeing across the moor. The ridge twists and narrows from the Hurkling Stones (hurkling means bending or crouching) and walkers are obliged to depart from the ridge path at Whinstone Lee Tor, despite the inviting southward continuation of the ridge path over Lead Hill. Follow the clear path that slips down to the wall beneath the edge going right to join the Moscar footpath which veers through a gateway and down the pasture to a gated lane beside a small plantation. Soon to ford Grindle Clough and pass between the rustic barns descending the pasture with the fence to the right swinging right to the stile onto the reservoir road (next to the road gate). Go right, rounding Mill Brook Bay, here anglers now cast where sad Derwent languishes beneath the road proceeds pleasantly back to Fairholme.

The Salt Cellar

WALK 11   STANAGE EDGE

from Hathersage
11½ miles

Hathersage is by repose the natural gateway to the High Peak. The name Hathersage does not mean 'heather's edge' but refers to Haver's or he-goats edge and probably is derived from the former name of Millstone Edge. The present settlement rests sweetly in the Derwent valley, formerly it clustering around the church upon Camp Green and originally was founded upon Hathersage Booths. actually under Millstone Edge.

The prime attraction for any visitor to the Hathersage locality must be Stanage Edge, the culmination of a long northern advancement of gritstone edges from Matlock. Here, rising in a wild moorland setting, in strong contrast to the Low Peak;   Kinder Scout, Bleaklow and Derwent Edge appear as dark brooding mountains whilst southwards stretches a pastoral peopled landscape of walls and green woods.

The vast majority of visitors ignore Hathersage as a walking base, preferring to drive up to either the Hollin Bank, Hook's Car or Surprise View car parks, or simply advance and backtrack from Moscar. However, the full merits of Stanage's situation are only disclosed to the walker who climbs from the depths of Derwent Dale and retreats to the sanctuary enriched by the more whole experience of moor and vale.

Carl Wark from Higger Tor

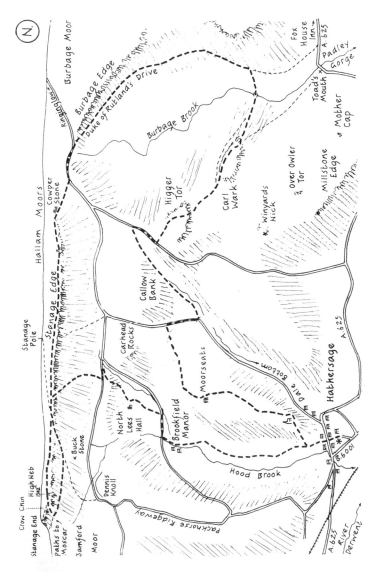

The Walk:

From the car park in the centre of the village, follow the alley north to cross the main road into Baulk Lane continuing on the clear track over a cattle grid and passing two isolated houses to a stile. Continue, crossing two more stiles, branching left in mid-pasture, to a third stile. A narrow enclosed path leads past Brookfield Manor, it enters a pasture and reaches the minor road at a gate. Go right diverging left up the metalled road by the camping site, which leads up to North Lees Hall. This property is owned by the National Park Authority and tenanted as a farm and guest house. It was probably built at the end of the sixteenth century by the Eyre family, who became estranged for their Roman Catholic beliefs and dismissed from the district by the fiercely and narrowly Protestant Derbyshire folk in the late 17th. C. The farm buildings are 17th C. and include the remains of a Roman Catholic chapel built in 1685 only to be sacked in 1688.

North Lees Hall

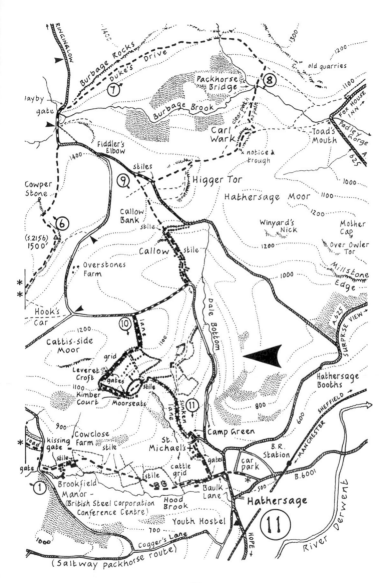

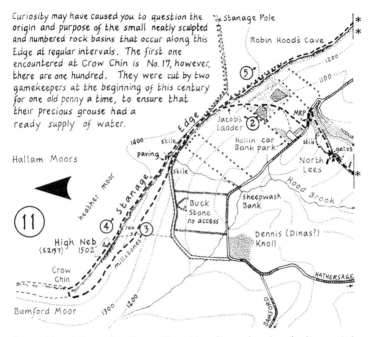

Curiosity may have caused you to question the origin and purpose of the small neatly sculpted and numbered rock basins that occur along this Edge at regular intervals. The first one encountered at Crow Chin is No. 17, however, there are one hundred. They were cut by two gamekeepers at the beginning of this century for one old penny a time, to ensure that their precious grouse had a ready supply of water.

Passing through two gates, follow the path up the pasture to enter the wooded environs of a cascading stream. On reaching the old turnpike road that ran from Ashopton (now submerged under Ladybower Reservoir) to Sheffield, go left then after the toilet block cum mountain rescue post (MRP on map) diverge right, short of the Hollin Bank car park. A well used path mounts through Stanage Plantation to climb the Edge by the old paved trod colloquially known as Jacob's Ladder.

Follow the edge-top path left descending with the lane from Stanage Pole. Cross the ladder stile beneath the Edge and hold to the path through the heather. Glancing left a large solitary boulder may be seen lower down the hillside, this is known as the Buck Stone. In the days when packhorsemen regulary trekked across these inhospitable moors this stone served as a vital staging post and refuge (the beam slots of the simple shelter may still be seen in the sides of the rock), and no doubt these hardy men often had cause to halt here, to sup their gin and rest their mules. The names Cogman, Cogger and Jagger often crop up in this district for they are associated with the packhorse trading days.

94

The path leading under High Neb is littered with partially fashioned mill-stones. The curiously named Crow Chin, supposedly arose from the apparition of a millstone cutter, who mistook the protruding rock for the beak of a giant crow bearing down upon him. The path wends on to meet the A.57 at Moscar, but walkers should seek the grassy ramp onto the Edge to backtrack for High Neb.

The popularity of this promenade is easily understood for the marvellously spacious view is a rich reward for what can be so little effort. Beyond High Neb notice the worn paving that appears to plummet over the edge, for this is the remains of the old packhorse route leading by the Buck Stone that has suffered quarry severance.

Keep with the edge-top path over a ladder stile and across the track, which is not on the original line of the Roman Long Causeway route: this possibly descended diagonally south more in accord with the present Jacob's Ladder path. The cliff becomes increasingly impressive and frequently adorned by a jingling array of rock-climbing talent. The Robin Hood's Cave balcony is certainly worth inspecting. Whether that legendary champion ever resorted to this exposed hideaway may not be proved but it seems quite plausible.

Passing the O.S. column the outcropping diminishes and concludes at the Cowper Stone. However, the path is guided away from this rock by a fence and crosses the wet moor to the Ringinglow road. Go forward with the road to seek the gate beyond the second bridge. Here join the Duke of Rutland's Drive, a green road running a gentle course under Burbage Rocks. Diverge from the track just before the small rocky cutting, descending on a clear path to the packhorse bridge across Burbage Brook. The path climbs diagonally to the depression beyond Carl Wark, but walkers should take the trouble to explore this ancient bastion by branching off the path and clambering round to the prow (southern approach), traversing to the great wall defending the only weakness on this prized natural stronghold.

View north-west from Stanage Edge

LOSE HILL PIKE   WIN HILL PIKE   KINDER SCOUT

BLEAKLOW HEAD

BAMFORD MOOR

The ridge path now addresses Higger (higher) Tor, which is well seen from Carl Wark, in particular the huge leaning tower on its western flank. Climb the pronounced ridge and trend right descending to the stile onto the road. Turn right to the stile on the left to descend with a thin path leading down the valley beneath Callow Bank (cold hill bank) to a stile into a walled lane. Ascending to the road, go right uphill to the lane going left. Where this swings north there opens a 'surprise' western view, featuring the Lose Hill ridge backed by Kinder Scout, with Hope and Derwent valleys below.

The lane proceeds by Leveret Croft to Kimber Court, where a gate puts the walker onto a fieldpath above Moorseats, which figures along with North Lees Hall in Charlotte Brontë's novel 'Jane Eyre'. This book was conceived from a three week stay at Hathersage made by Charlotte in 1845.

At the corresponding stile the route enters a lane passing Carhead. Two shorter footpaths are mapped, the one from Toothill Farm joins the lane just prior to it becoming a sunken, though well surfaced, lane leading down the ridge by Camp Green (site of a circular encampment surrounded by a ditch) to enter St. Michael's churchyard through the lych gate. Allow time to inspect Little John's Grave and the predominantly 14th & 15th C. church which contains not only a chancel window rescued from the submerged Derwent parish church but also several fine brasses of the Eyre family. The route departs from the churchyard descending by a wall to re-enter Baulk Lane and Hathersage main street.

GRADIENT PROFILE

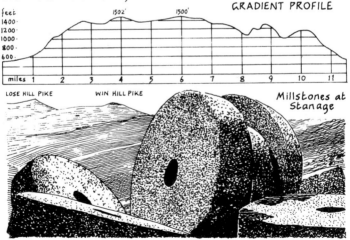

Millstones at Stanage

High Neb

Robin Hood's Balcony, Stanage Edge

HIGH NEB

MAM TOR   BACK TOR   LOSE HILL PIKE

Twitchell Farm

WALK 12

from Hope

WIN HILL PIKE

5 miles

Win Hill Pike makes a delightful half day excursion and whilst there are several interesting lines of ascent certainly that via Twitchell Farm is the most pleasant. At the opposite extreme the route from Yorkshire Bridge via Parkin Clough is indubitably a real horror, a muddy step ladder under a heavy canopy of conifers.

Geographically, Win Hill belongs to the Kinder Scout massif, but the long connecting ridge, forming a curtain barrier between the Woodlands and Noe valleys, gives the hill a strong independence and may fairly claim to be one of the prime viewpoints of Peakland.

The Walk :

Start from the car park in Hope village beside the Woodroffe Arms, follow the minor road bound for Edale. Diverge right down the lane to Killhill Bridge,

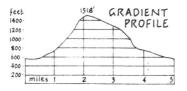

continuing with the lane passing under the railway, whereupon turn right to follow the track climbing to Twitchell Farm (which means 'steep path'). Beyond the farmyard ascend the steep pasture to a stile. A clear path advances onto (and across) the ridge: go right to mount the serrated

98

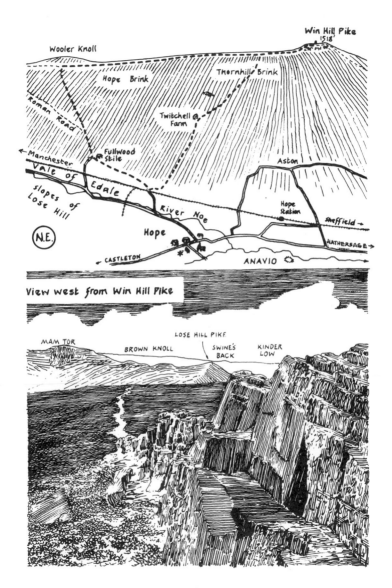

Win Hill Pike
1518'

Wooler Knoll

Hope Brink

Thornhill Brink

Roman Road

Twitchell Farm

← Manchester

Fullwood Stile

Aston

Vale of Edale

River Noe

slopes of Lose Hill

Hope Station

Sheffield →

N.E.

Hope

← CASTLETON

HATHERSAGE →

ANAVIO

View west from Win Hill Pike

MAM TOR

BROWN KNOLL

LOSE HILL PIKE

SWINE'S BACK

KINDER LOW

ridge onto Win Hill Pike. The name Win Hill has attracted many fanciful and unscholarly explanations though few pay heed to the earliest recorded references. In the late 13th C. it appears as 'Wythinehull' which meant 'withy' or 'willow hill', and despite the shroud of conifers there are fragments of willow in Win Hill Plantation even today.

Win Hill Pike is a real charmer of a summit offering a superb panorama plus a dash of scrambling to boot. Retrace steps from the O.S. column to pass the cross ridge path at the signpost, proceeding on the obvious ridgetop path, oddly not marked on Ordnance maps, gently declining towards Wooler Knoll. There are several references to wild animals in the place-names of High Peak and Wooler Knoll must have been the lofty retreat of wolves. Just subsequent to the cross ridge wall branch left down the bridleway (enjoying the fine views of the Vale of Edale and Kinder Scout from this green track) which descends to join the Roman Road track just prior to the gate into the lane leading down to Fullwood Stile Farm. Pass through the farmyard and cross the stile following the hedgeline south, maintaining course with the legionary street to regain the railway underpass beyond The Homestead, and so return to Hope along the road as the excursion began.

Win Hill Pike

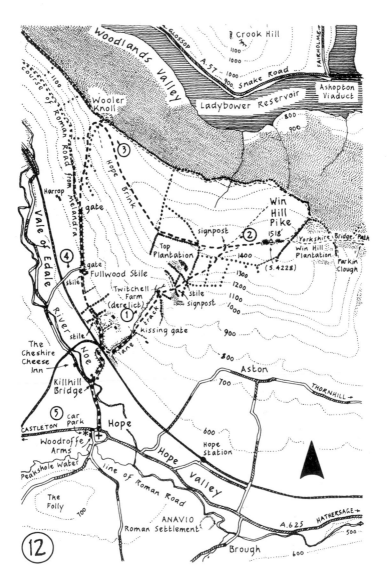

Crook Hill

Woodlands Valley

GLOSSOP

A.57

Snake Road

FAIRHOLME

Ashopton Viaduct

Ladybower Reservoir

Wooler Knoll

course of Roman Road from Melandra

Harrop

Hope Brink

gate

③

Vale of Edale

④

gate
Fullwood Stile
stile

Twitchell Farm
(derelict)

①

stile

kissing gate

lane

stile

Top Plantation

signpost

②

Win Hill Pike
1518'

(S.4228)

Yorkshire Bridge Path
Win Hill Plantation

Parkin Clough

signpost
stile

River Noe

The Cheshire Cheese Inn

Killhill Bridge

⑤

car park

Aston

THORNHILL

CASTLETON

Hope

Woodroffe Arms

Peakshole Water

line of Roman Road

Hope Valley

Hope Station

The Folly

ANAVIO
Roman Settlement

A.625

HATHERSAGE

Brough

⑫

Chapter Four

Back Tor

Kinder Scout has long held a very special place in the affections of Manchester and Sheffield ramblers.

About the turn of the century the growing desire to explore the wild places near to these vast urban industrialised centres inevitably concentrated on the High Peak moors, and with the forcing through of the Cowburn tunnel the railway focussed attention on Edale and the impressive crag rimmed plateau of Kinder Scout in particular.   But access was severely restricted and it took actions like the Mass Trespass of 1932 to bring to the broader public attention the ludicrous state of affairs that allowed a few wealthy grouse-moor owners the exclusive right to ban public access.

It has taken many years and the gentling hand of the National Park Authority to administer a workable open country compromise, this operating today under the keen eye of the Ranger Service.

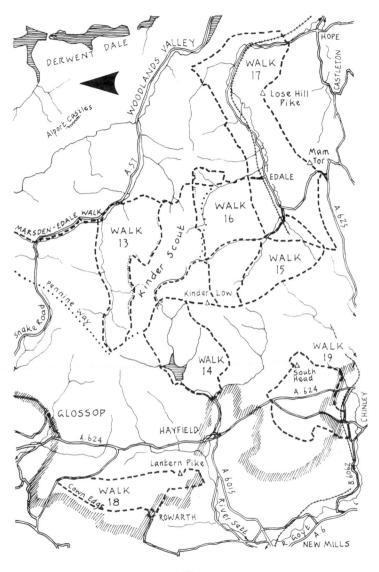

DERWENT DALE

WOODLANDS VALLEY

Alport Castles

A.57

MARSDEN-EDALE WALK

Snake Road

Pennine Way

WALK 13

Kinder Scout

WALK 16

Kinder Low △

WALK 14

WALK 17

△ Lose Hill Pike

EDALE

Mam △ Tor

A.625

WALK 15

HOPE

CASTLETON

WALK 19

△ South Head

A.624

CHINLEY

B.6062

GLOSSOP

A.624

HAYFIELD

Lantern Pike △

WALK 18

Cown Edge

ROWARTH

A.6015

River Sett

R. Goyt

A.6

NEW MILLS

103

WALK 13

KINDER SCOUT
SEAL and ASHOP EDGES

from the Snake Inn

9¼ miles

The northern edges of Kinder Scout provide one of the most rewarding and dramatic walks in the High Peak. From the depths of the upper Woodlands Valley the route climbs steeply onto Seal Edge parading along the craggy rim by Chinese Wall, Fairbrook Naze, Black Ashop Edge and the curious Boxing Glove Rocks descending to Ashop Head to return down the Snake Path.

Whilst the majority of walkers are drawn 'like bees round a honey pot' to Kinder Downfall, a comparatively few venture above these furthest shadowy walls and clefts, a fact that advances the virtues of this expedition.

The route is measured from the Snake Inn, but as the Inn's car park is definitely for patrons only, walkers are advised to park at Birchin Clough, necessitating tracking down the Lady Clough Forest Trail to the River Ashop to commence the walk and eventually backtrack.

Boxing Gloves Rocks

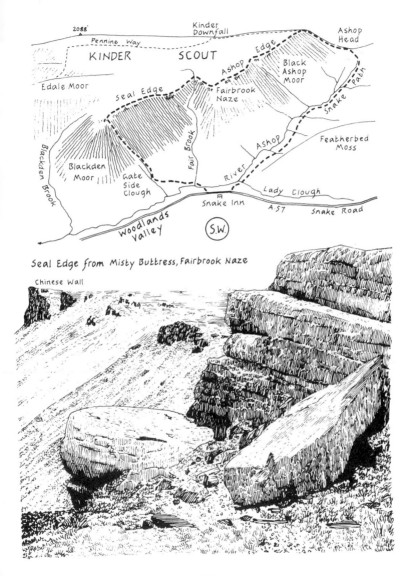

Seal Edge from Misty Buttress, Fairbrook Naze

Chinese Wall

The Walk :

Go down the A.57 from the Snake Inn locating the signposted path right through the thin belt of conifers to a footbridge across the River Ashop. The hillside rising to the right bears the name Nungrain Brink, which is a lingering record that the Nuns of St. Mary's in Derby held land here in the early 13th.C.

There is a clear path forking right to climb above Fair Brook, and left to seek an awkward crossing of that stream. The route takes the latter course mounting quite steeply on a well marked path into Gate Side Clough (the word Gate is here a reference to some former valley track no longer discernible. This present path probably came into being to service the shooting butts. It soon becomes indistinct rising with the broken wall and is lost as the route ascends to the brink at Seal Stones. There, joining the beater's path, go right.

Navigation henceforward is determined by the vagaries of the Edge, any elaborate description would merely serve to confuse. Suffice it to say that despite the eroded peat the next four miles are a sheer delight and should not be hurried. The natural route from Fair Brook to Kinder Downfall has been plotted for those walkers who cannot resist visiting that arena of the multitudes. The prime way retains company with the Edge and to admire Chinese Wall and gaze from Fairbrook Naze (nose) to survey the wild expanse of Featherbed Moss, Bleaklow and the upper Derwent moors and edges. Advancing along Black Ashop Edge ('Black' because of its northern aspect) the outcropping peters out from the Boxing Gloves and the route finally quits the plateau rim above Mill Hill Rocks down to Ashop Head'. This steep descent briefly accompanies the Pennine Way which helps to explain the poor state of the path, so minimise soil disturbance by descending with caution.

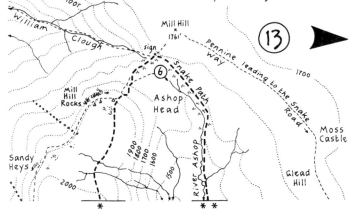

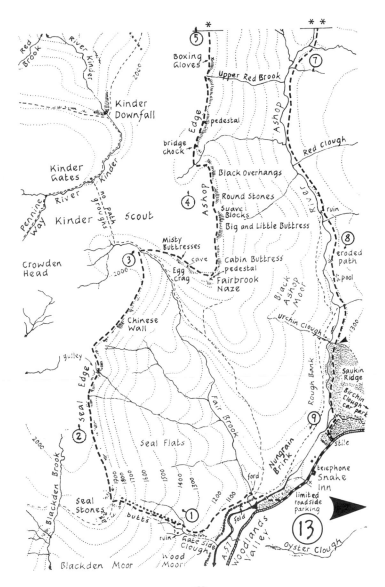

Red Brook
River Kinder
2000
Kinder Downfall
Kinder Gates
Kinder River
Pennine Way
Kinder Scout
no path groughs
Crowden Head
Misty Buttresses
③ cave
Egg Crag
2000
Chinese Wall
gulley
Seal Edge
② 2000
Blackden Brook
Seal Flats
Seal Stones
butts
2000 1800 1700 1600 1500 1400 1300
① 1200 1100
ruin
Gate Side Clough
Wood Moor
Blackden Moor

* ⑤
Boxing Gloves
Upper Red Brook
⑦
Edge
pedestal
bridge chock
Black Overhangs
Round Stones
④ Ashop
Suave Blocks
Big and Little Buttress
Cabin Buttress
pedestal
Fairbrook Naze
Ashop
Red Clough
River Ashop
ruin
⑧
eroded path
pool
Black Ashop Moor
Urchin Clough
Rough Bank
Saukin Ridge
Birchin Clough Car Park
⑨
stile
Fair Brook
Nungrain Brink
telephone
Snake Inn
ford
limited roadside parking
⑬
fold
A57
Woodlands Valley
Oyster Clough

107

Black Ashop Edge

From the signpost where the Pennine Way and the Snake Path cross, go right, to descend from Ashop Head with the clear track. This old path must have gained its present name from the passage of Hayfield folk into the Woodlands Valley, on specific occasion to the Alport 'Love Feast'.

The path down the head stream of the Woodlands is far from an anti-climax, for it twists and turns in sympathy with the infant Ashop (which means 'ash-tree valley') through grough and eroded earth bank profiles. Lower down as the valley constricts, with the path well above the stream, an awkward landslipped section calls for a wary eye and a cautious step. Soon the path enters the Lady Clough Plantations under Saukin Ridge descending to cross the Lady Clough footbridge from where the Snake Inn (right) and Birchin Clough car park (left) are easily reached.

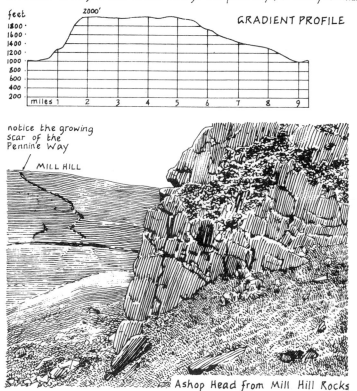

GRADIENT PROFILE

feet
2000'
1800 ·
1600 ·
1400 ·
1200 ·
1000 ·
800 ·
600 ·
400 ·
200 ·
miles 1   2   3   4   5   6   7   8   9

notice the growing scar of the Pennine Way

MILL HILL

Ashop Head from Mill Hill Rocks

109

WALK 14   KINDER DOWNFALL

from the Sett Valley

6¾ miles

It is a commonly held misconception that the High Peak is composed of bleak boggy boring moorland redeemed but briefly from eternal damnation by Kinder Downfall. Indeed, the considerable virtues of this high country have been little advanced by the Pennine Way's too-hasty flight from the Peak District, creating in its wake a linear laceration of raw peat across the moors.

So many heavily laden Pennine Wayfarers 'perplexed and bemused' pass by the Downfall grim faced as a result of the problems of the Kinder plateau at such an early stage in their marathon and it is no wonder. To really enjoy Kinder Downfall then it should be treated as the culmination of a days ramble, preferably from the Sett Valley, above Hayfield, thereby embracing it rather than giving it a passing glance.

The Downfall is a place of common resort, though only after a period of rain does the waterfall, at nearly 100 feet the tallest in Peakland, really show its stature. Few walkers do not allow time to peruse the impressive amphitheatre of weathered gritstone. It is fascinating to learn of the origins and career of this coarse rock, for although it lies pancake flat 2000 feet up, it was formed as an extensive sandbank at sea level and became buried beneath Coal Measures down to a depth of 5000 feet. Then, from some 290 million years ago the area became subject to the tremendous Hercynian mountain building forces which progressively raised the earth several thousand feet to create the Pennine chain. Erosive forces quickly denuded the overlying coal (and the gritstone from southern Peakland), so the present general surface was established possibly 220 million years ago.

Rocks on The Three Knolls

110

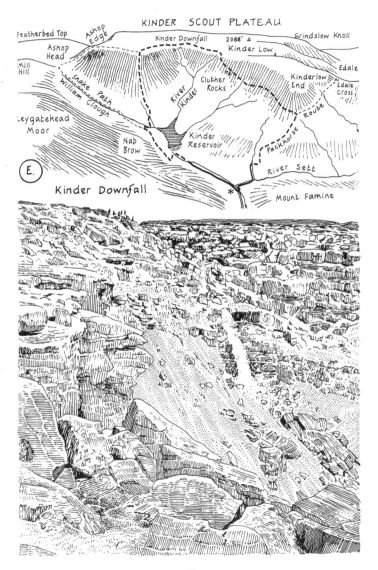

KINDER SCOUT PLATEAU

Featherbed Top · Ashop Edge · Kinder Downfall · 2088' △ · Grindslow Knoll
Ashop Head · Kinder Low
Mill Hill
Snake Path · William Clough · River Kinder · Cluther Rocks · Kinderlow End · Edale · Edale Cross
Leygatehead Moor · Packhorse Route
Nab Brow · Kinder Reservoir
River Sett
Kinder Downfall · Mount Famine

(E.)

Kinder Downfall

111

The Walk:

This advance is deemed to start from the Bowden Bridge car park near the confluence of the rivers Kinder and Sett, though this parking facility is notoriously quick to fill on any fine weekend - forcing many visitors to resort to the larger car park back in the village of Hayfield.

This old quarry featured in the famous Mass Trespass on Kinder in 1932 (see memorial plaque on quarry wall). Follow the minor road from Bowden Bridge beside the River Sett leading up to Tunstead Clough Farm, passing round the farm buildings as the farmer's waymarks bid.

Originally this farm served as a staging post on the packhorse trade route from Lancashire and Cheshire over into Edale bound for the Yorkshire markets. Proceed uphill on the farm track then swing right locating three kissing gates onto the recently cultivated Harry Moor. Follow the wall uphill to a ladder stile continuing to the cross-path beneath the steep rise of Kinderlow End. From the gate posts in the broken wall advance upon the rising path on course for the Three Knolls.

The path crosses a depression and mounts well above Cluther Rocks: however the illustrated route slants across to explore the Rocks seeking the few partially hewn millstones that rest among the confusion of boulders. The long ascent to the Edge concludes at the rocky head of Red Brook (here joining the Pennine Way alternative), running along the increasingly impressive Edge to Kinder Downfall. The Downfall is a monumental and profound ravine; unrivalled in the High Peak and fully deserving its popular appeal, indeed it is the focus of the overwhelming majority of expeditions upon Kinder Scout. Whilst Kinder Scout may rise abruptly from Edale to establish the highest ground in all Peakland there is hardly a summit worthy of the name. Instead walkers turn their peak-bagging instincts across (or round) the expansive plateau to gather in gregarious profusion about this perilous Edge, consuming sandwiches and chocolate bars (many thoughtlessly discarding orange peel and worse), then make tracks for the valley well satisfied with this less orthodox accomplishment.

The strong westerly gales that frequently bombard and besiege this plateau Edge have a knack of raising the overspilling moorland stream into a plume of spray, depositing it far back upon the rocks and, of course, upon any hapless soul unwary of this eventuality - watch out for those sudden up-draughts!

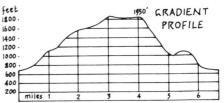

GRADIENT PROFILE

1950'

112

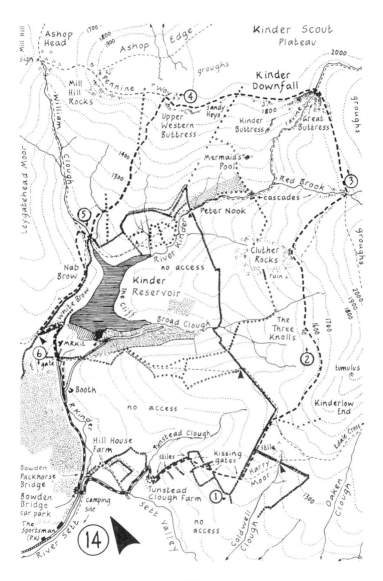

Mill Hill

Ashop Head
sign ×

1700
1800
1900

Ashop Edge

groughs

Kinder Scout
Plateau

2000

Kinder
Downfall

Pennine Way
④

Mill
Hill
Rocks

Upper
Western
Buttress

sandy
Heys

1800

Kinder
Buttress

ravine

Great
Buttress

groughs

William Clough

1400

1300

Mermaid's
Pool

Red Brook

cascades

③

Leygatehead Moor

⑤

Peter Nook

River Kinder

no access

Cluther
Rocks

ruin

groughs

2000

1900

Nab
Brow

Kinder
Reservoir

The Cliff

Broad Clough

The
Three
Knolls

1600

1700

1800

White Brow

MRKiL

②

tumulus

⑥

gate

Booth

no access

Kinderlow
End

Eccles Cross

R Kinder

Hill House
Farm

Tunstead Clough

stiles

kissing
gates

stile

Harry
Moor

1300

Oaken Clough

Bowden
Packhorse
Bridge

Bowden
Bridge
car park

camping
site

Tunstead
Clough Farm

①

sett Valley

no
access

Coldwell Clough

The
Sportsman
(P.H.)

River Sett

⑭

There are several exciting viewpoints from which to admire Kinder Downfall, though extreme caution must always be employed by camera enthusiasts seeking dramatic shots and novice scramblers attempting to find (non-existent) easy ways down into the ravine.

The Edge path by Sandy Heys crosses much sadly denuded peat, an emphatic reminder of the all too frequent peat fires that can smoulder for days, even weeks. These destructive fires, the annual nightmare of Park Rangers, farmers and firemen alike, ravage the peat landscape accelerating its demise. Walkers must carry the principal burden of blame for these fires - please heed warnings of tinder dry conditions which can exist at any time from early May and persist for long periods throughout the summer months - don't let any fire arise from your thoughtlessness!

Whilst it has long been the common practice to continue above the western buttresses and descend the steep and scarred path to Ashop Head there joining the Snake Path by turning left into William Clough the upper grainings of which have also suffered scouring erosion from walkers. The route here advised avoids unnecessarily exacerbating these problem paths by taking an earlier line of descent from Upper Western Buttress. Initially there is little sign of a path but from the 1600 foot contour one transpires bringing the walker surely down to the foot of William Clough just above the reservoir enclosure wall. Go right to join the Snake Path rising with it left onto Nab Brow. If you started from Hayfield then retain the Snake Path, otherwise follow the zig-zagging path with the wall above the dam to the gate next to the entrance of the Water Board filtration plant. Cross the footbridge and follow the path beside the River Kinder, thence conclude along the road, passing, by the confluence of the Kinder with the Sett, a slender packhorse footbridge.

Keen eyes will notice that the path up the River Kinder from the reservoir has been shown. Whilst this magnificent approach to the Downfall (a scramblers route can be located on the northern flank of the ravine not far from the waterfall) is frequently used, notably by rock-climbers, it is not a right of way nor an access point. The Water Board have no strong objections to the use of the section from the foot of William Clough through their enclosure, however, between the points marked A - A, the path crosses private non-access land belonging to Kinder Estates, and should therefore be respected as such.

S.W. from Sandy Heys

114

Kinder Downfall

The Mermaid's Pool looking to Red Brook

The Kinder River at Peter Nook Wood

Kinder River and Downfall

WALK 15   KINDER DOWNFALL
from Edale

8½ miles

Whilst this outing shares a common objective with WALK 14 any further resemblance ceases there. For one thing Kinder Downfall is reached in blind faith, being totally obscured until the last moment, there is also a greater diversity of scenery with an earnest piece of grough navigation to spice the whole experience.

There are few better places to marshal and gain a competence with the ground rules of sound compass work than on the infamous Kinder plateau. Any mist can bring immediate confusion and dismay if the walker does not frequently relate the map to the ground and vice versa – a procedure that must become habit and be applied equally in clear weather as in deteriorating conditions. The perplexing maze of grough channels, that have defied faithful representation on the popular O.S. mapping scales, make bee-line navigation very difficult, but far from impossible. Positive compass control coupled with swift remedial action when an awkward grough sequence forces some deviation will enable targets to be achieved with efficiency providing you have complete confidence in the infallibility of a properly used compass.

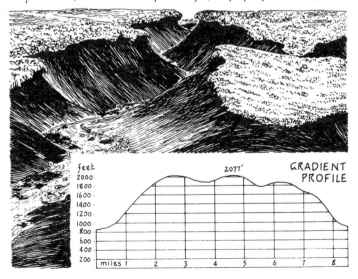

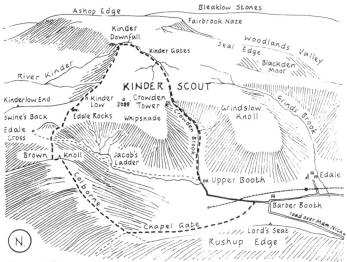

Ashop Edge · Bleaklow Stones · Fairbrook Naze · Kinder Downfall · Kinder Gates · Seal Edge · Woodlands Valley · River Kinder · Blackden Moor · KINDER SCOUT · Kinderlow End · Kinder Low 2088 · Crowden Tower · Grindslow Knoll · Grinds Brook · Swine's Back · Edale Rocks · Whipsnade · Crowden Brook · Edale Cross · Brown Knoll · Jacob's Ladder · Upper Booth · Edale · Colborne · Barber Booth · road over Mam Nick · Chapel Gate · Lord's Seat · Rushup Edge · N.

The Walk :

From the car park above Barber Booth, follow the minor road to Upper Booth passing down to a stile beside Crowden Brook road bridge.   A clear path proceeds upstream to a footbridge, entering open country at a stile.

A path from Broadlee Bank joins the valley path as it climbs steadily up this delightfully secluded clough.   Progress can be quite swift till the cascades at the head of the ravine hamper the way calling for some caution. Once at the lip of the ravine go forward with the principal stream, paying particular attention to your compass across Crowden Head, on a course seeking the main feeder of the River Kinder (N.N.W. of the point of entry onto the moor).   This section is busy with deep drain- age channels (locally known as 'groughs') and the discovery of Kinder Gates, especially in poor visibility, is a cause of relief and the spectral state of 'being lost' is extinguished from the mind.   The moorland stream has by now gained greater definition running a broad course, in a sandy bed. Soon to sweep westward to plunge over the lip of the moor at Kinder Downfall.

There is no other waterfall to match this in all Peakland, the name Downfall is most appropriate conjuring up graphic images of a chaos of sheer rock and wildly careering white water, which accurately describes this crag- bound spectacle. However, problems arise when determining the name Kinder, whilst 'Scout' appears to derive from the Old Norse 'skuti' meaning 'lofty overhanging rock', which clearly relates to the rocky

119

amphitheatre when viewed from below. 'Kinder' submits to no such easy etymological answer. In the Domesday Survey of 1086, it appears as 'Chendre' and place-name scholars believe it to be an obscure pre-English hill-name which parallels with the modern Welsh 'Cynwyd-fre' and therefore identical to the first element in Countisbury, in Devon.

The route departs southwards along the sloping peat fringed Edge by Red Brook, with the path on a broad front to Kinder Low. Beyond the triangulation column an excavated tumulus seems to have eluded Ordnance Surveyors, is this not the 'Low' of Kinder Low?

The unmistakable path of the masses leads past Edale Rocks, which offer some shelter from prevailing south-westerlies, and on across grotesquely burnt peat to the broken wall and down from beneath the Swine's Back to the signpost. Consider now your available time, as the packhorse track down into Edale, via Jacob's Ladder, is your only option hereon until Chapel Gate. The ridge route accompanies the wall, veering left at the dike to attain the summit of Brown Knoll.

The clearly defined ridge path has long served as the natural high level link on the popular Edale Horseshoe and Derwent Watershed Walks, but has not received formal recognition as a right-of-way, therefore, you pass this way only by the good grace of the landowners!

Advance along the Colborne edge to the large cairn where Chapel Gate is joined, going left diagonally down the steep flank of Lord's Seat. The name Chapel Gate derives from it being the old road to Chapel-en-le-Frith. A well marked path leads through the enclosures and beside the farm buildings of Manor House farm to the valley by-road, turning left to regain the point of departure, going under the grandly arched railway bridge.

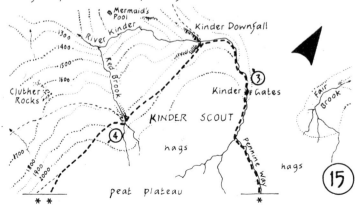

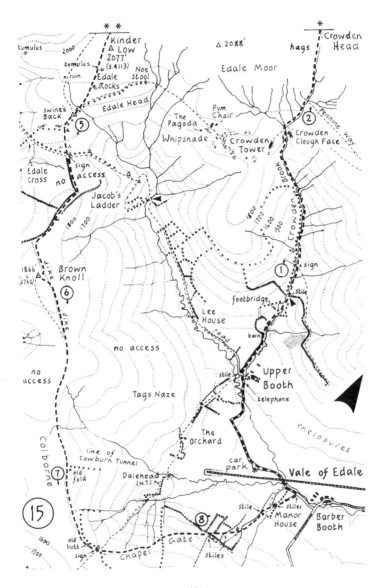

Kinder Low △ 2077' (s.4113)

tumulus 2000

tumulus

x ruin

Edale Rocks

Noe Stool

swine's Back ⑤

Edale Head

△ 2088'

hags **Crowden Head**

Edale Moor

Pym Chair

The Pagoda

Whipsnade **Crowden Tower**

Crowden Clough Face ②

Pennine Way

Edale Cross

sign no access

Jacob's Ladder

1800 1700

Crowden Brook

1800 1700 1600

1500

① sign

footbridge

stile

dike Brown Knoll 1866 △ 2762'

⑥

dike

no access

Lee House

road

barn

no access

no access

Tags Naze

stile

Upper Booth

telephone

enclosures

Colborne

line of Cowburn Tunnel

⑦ old fold

Dalehead (N.T.)

The Orchard

car park

Vale of Edale

⑮

old butt sign

Chapel

Gate

stile

stiles

Manor House

Barber Booth

1600

1500

stiles

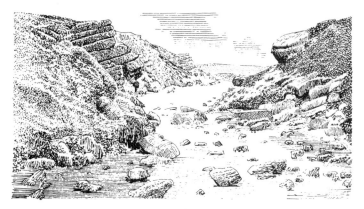

Kinder Gates

Kinder Downfall

Crowden Tower from the head of Crowden Clough

Edale Rocks

WALK 16   KINDER SCOUT
THE SOUTHERN EDGES

from Edale   8¼ miles

Since the designation of the Pennine Way starting at Edale (instead of Ashbourne, the more logical springboard), there has been an explosion of recreational activity from the mid-1960's. This has wrought considerable havoc with the surface of numerous sensitive paths on Kinder Scout; as will be immediately apparent to anyone who sets his course up Grinds Brook. Upon the moor the most tangible effect has been the deterioration of the Edges path.

Whilst it is considered that the blanket peat, through a range of climatic and landuse factors, has been undergoing an irreversible degeneration for many years, damage from recreational use is becoming of major consequence.

The lateral exaggeration of the Edges path, reflecting an inevitable concentration on the most obviously scenic parts will not diminish unless possibly unpopular localised action is taken to curb the worst effects of vibrams upon the bare peat and tenuous vegatative cover. Resources, manpower and the best answers to secure a durable trod are not in abundance - clearly this is a cause of greater concern to all who genuinely wish to protect and enjoy these beautiful wild moors, than simply demanding more access elsewhere.

The walk illustrated here does not embrace the entire southern Edges of Kinder but takes the more direct line of approach via Ringing Roger. Walkers of more independent natures are at liberty to proceed east via Rowland Cote to ascend Jaggers Clough or to advance to the Roman Road branching onto open country in the vicinity of Blackley Clough, to bring Crookstone Knoll and the curiously named boundary rocks of Madwoman's Stones underfoot.

There are two grand circular walks frequently undertaken from Edale, the Edale Horseshoe and the Kinder Edges walk (a complete tour round the plateau rim): these fit into the 'big walk' bracket demanding plenty of daylight to accomplish.

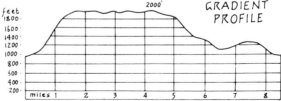

GRADIENT PROFILE

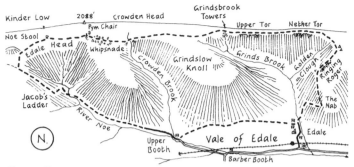

The walk:

From the large car park below Edale station, go up the road under the railway bridge passing through Grindsbrook Booth by the Old Nags Head. Follow the Pennine Way crossing the footbridge in the Grinds Brook dingle, diverging right up the pasture from the main valley path to an access point stile.

A zig-zagging path leads up onto The Nab, which is an excellent viewpoint, then aims north through the heather to mount the rocky spine of Ringing Roger. This name embodies two old words describing these prominent rocks, the latter being a corruption of Rocher, as in The Roaches WALK 22.

On my last visit an alcove cairn stood upon the burnt peat above the rocks but as cairns are exposed more to the whims of visitors than the elements it may not survive long. Work round the head of Golden Clough onto the fraying peaty fringe above Nether Tor. The views easily compensate for the poor state of the path, with Grinds Brook far below and exciting crags lining the Edge sustaining interest.

The most impressive part of Grinds Brook, from which it may have derived its name 'Grim's Brook' - the devil's ravine - occurs where the stream spills off the moor. The stream cascades beneath the sheer walls of Grinds Brook Towers. The route veers north to accommodate this deep ravine, then contours south and swings west crossing the Pennine Way steering for the head of Crowden Brook. Retain the path rising south onto Crowden Tower, a notable vantage point, before aiming west again to encounter a confused mass of weathered gritstone boulders and blocks, whimsically referred to as Whipsnade - an analogy derived from the weird likeness to zoo animals achieved by some individual stones. They are more properly known as The Woolpacks and time is well spent exploring their many and varied grotesque forms. The Edges path continues to the Pagoda, rocks that rise in near true definition as a many-storeyed tapering tower. Standing nearby is Pym Chair, an outcast from the Boxing Glove Stones across the moor on Black Ashop Edge.

125

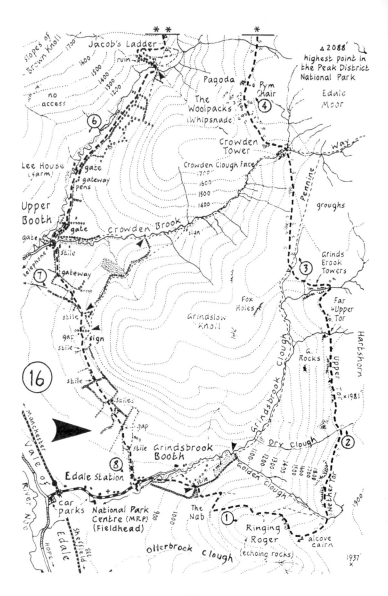

slopes of Brown Knoll
1700
1600
1500
1400
1300
1200

* *

Jacob's Ladder

ruin

no access

⑥

Pagoda

The Woolpacks (Whipsnade)

*

△ 2088′ highest point in the Peak District National Park

Pym Chair

④

Edale Moor

Crowden Tower

Crowden Clough Face
1700
1600
1500
1400

Pennine Way

groughs

Lee House (farm)

gate
gateway
pens

Upper Booth

gate

gate

Crowden Brook

sign

Grinds Brook Towers

③

gateway

telephone

stile

⑦

Far Upper Tor

Fox Holes

Grindslow Knoll

G. Rocks

Upper Tor

Hartshorn

stile
gap
stile
sign

×1981

⑯

stile

stiles

gap

stile

Grindsbrook Booth

Dry Clough

②

Grindsbrook Clough

Golden Clough

Nether Tor

1100
1200
1300
1400
1500
1600
1700
1800

Netherhand

900

⑧

Edale Station

stile

car parks

National Park Centre (MRP) (Fieldhead)

+

1000

The Nab

①

Ringing Roger (echoing rocks)

alcove cairn

1937 ×

Manchester

Vale of

River Noe

Edale

HOPE

Ollerbrook Clough

Youngate Bridge

The route descends the wet depression about the headwaters of the
River Noe to rise to the Noe Stool, a giant anvil shaped rock, then
follows the broken wall under Swine's Back, descending the spongy moor
to join the packhorse track. Go left with the stony way, heeding the
notice a little over half way down imploring walkers not to continue straight
down the landslipped bank. Instead, either go left with the stony track
or right along a grassy bridleway which becomes a walled lane leading
down to Youngate Bridge, thus avoiding the unstable ground on the other
Jacob's Ladder routes. This charming footbridge is a rare survivor from
the days of cogman and jaggers. An obvious track leads down the valley
by Lee House (National Trust property) to Upper Booth (formerly Crowdenlee Booth).
Pass through the farmyard adhering to the well marked footpath across Broadlee
Bank to re-enter Grindsbrook Booth opposite the Old Nag's Head - how
convenient!

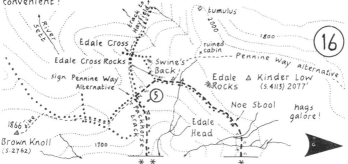

127

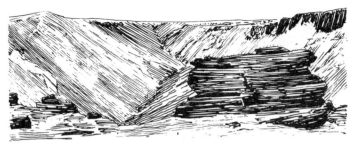

Upper Grindsbrook Clough from Ringing Roger (the echoing rocks)

Grindsbrook Towers looking to The Fox Holes and Grindslow Knoll

Pym Chair
and
Noe Stool

The Woolpacks (whimsically known as Whipsnade or the Mushroom Garden)

SWINE'S
BACK

EDALE
CROSS

EDALE
ROCKS

The Great Ridge from Lord's Seat

WALK 17 — THE GREAT RIDGE

from Mam Nick

14¼ miles

There are very few real ridge walks in Peakland, and certainly no other quite so interesting as the Lose Hill - Lord's Seat ridge, frequently referred to as the Great Ridge, which runs for four miles east to west. It plays an important role for the spectator, striking a contrasting divide between the ancient carboniferous limestone uplands of Low Peak and the generally higher gritstone plateau. This juxtaposition is seen best from the vantage point provided by the summit of Mam Tor - the 'Mother' and 'Shivering' mountain. It further acts as an embracing arm confining the Vale of Edale, creating a sanctuary in the hills ; though packhorse trails and later road and railway links contrived over the years to open up this sheltered community.

Much of the Great Ridge is notoriously prone to landslipping. The east face of Mam Tor and the north face of Back Tor being the most manifest proof, whilst the hummocky northern flanks of Lord's Seat show an earlier phase of instability which was triggered off following periglacial periods with melt water flushing the valleys.

The walk described here is a happy combination of airy ridge and gentle valley paths, with numerous opportunties to curtail the excursion or to extend it by continuing along the Roman Road to the access point onto Crookstone Hill, turning it into a full high-level circuit of Edale by ascending to Crookstone Knoll and Madwoman's Stones joining WALK 16 and linking over Brown Knoll WALK 15 to the head of Chapel Gate.

130

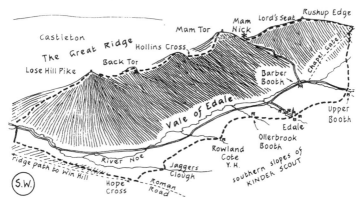

The map illustration is labelled with: Castleton, The Great Ridge, Hollins Cross, Back Tor, Lose Hill Pike, Mam Tor, Mam Nick, Lord's Seat, Rushup Edge, Chapel Gate, Barber Booth, Upper Booth, Edale, Ollerbrook Booth, Vale of Edale, Rowland Cote Y.H., River Noe, Jaggers Clough, southern slopes of KINDER SCOUT, ridge path to Win Hill, Hope Cross, Roman Road, S.W.

The Walk:

From the large car park off the A.625 beneath Mam Nick, walk up to the pass climbing the steps onto Mam Tor summit. For such little effort this is a very rewarding viewpoint, notably of the southern aspect of Kinder Scout and a large portion of the Vale of Edale from Edale Head. Castleton, Peveril Castle and the amazing Winnats are also well seen to the south-east. It is important to show caution if you choose to inspect the giant eastern declivity, where the friable sandstones and shales are continually slipping away; fierce winds and the more dangerous surprise draught can expose the unwary onlooker to a potentially fatal fall!

Mam Tor has evidence of settlement as early as 1180 B.C. (late Bronze Age), though the visible defences were dug much later by Iron Age people, who lingered until the Roman seizure of the Peak District in the first century A.D. The fort enclosed an area of sixteen acres and when occupied the fearsome shattered cliff that gave the hill its alternative name 'the Shivering Mountain,' can hardly have begun undermining the hill.

The ridge path to Lose Hill Pike curves and dips to Hollins Cross, where there is a memorial topograph, then rises on the narrower ridge (with an optional contouring path) to descend to Back Tor Nook. The collapsed north-western flank makes a dramatic sight but Brockett Booth Plantation, which formerly gave the cliff a mysterious majesty, has withered to a tatty state.
The ridge path further detracts from the whole being badly worn - take care climbing up the unprotected edge. The ridge path finally is relieved of the wall on the rise onto Lose Hill Pike. Lose Hill (pronounced 'loose') appears to be a translocated name for it derives from the Old English word 'hlose' meaning pig-sty, which is hardly likely to have been sited near the top of the hill - a tentative alternative derivation might be 'lluest' Old Welsh for a 'booth'.

131

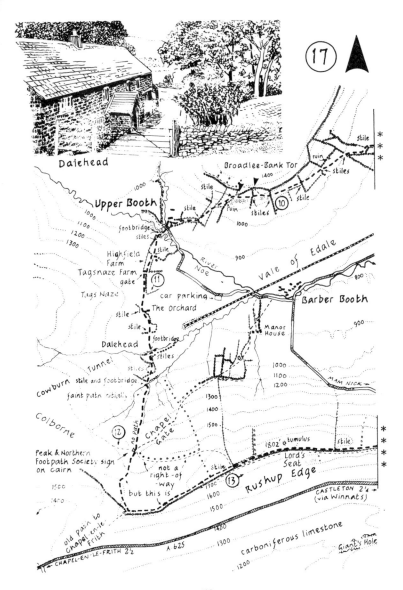

Dalehead

17

Broadlee-Bank Tor

stile

1400

ruin

stiles

stile

10

stile

ruin

stile

1000

Upper Booth

1000

stile

footbridge

stiles

1200

1300

River Noe

stile

900

Vale of Edale

800

Highfield Farm

11

Tagsnaze Farm gate

Tags Naze

car parking

The Orchard

Barber Booth

900

stile

stile

Manor House

footbridge

Dalehead

stiles

stiles

1000

1100

1200

MAM NICK

Tunnel

Cowburn stile and footbridge

faint path initially

1300

Colborne

1400

12

Chapel gate

1500

1802' tumulus

stile

Peak & Northern Footpath Society sign on cairn

not a right-of way but this is

stile

13

Lord's Seat

Rushup Edge

1500

1400

1700

1600

1500

CASTLETON 2¼ (via Winnats)

old path to Chapel-en-le-Frith

1400

carboniferous limestone

Giant's Hole

CHAPEL-EN-LE-FRITH 2½

A 625

1300

1200

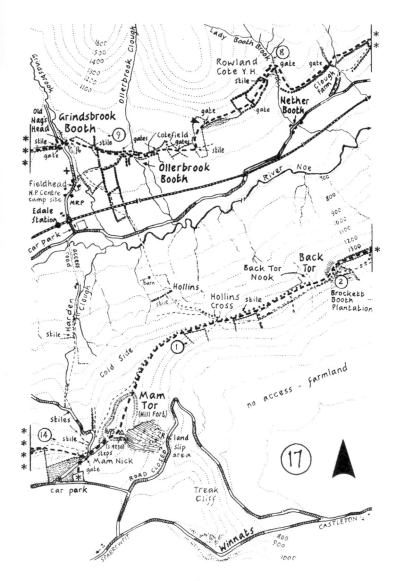

Maps mark the summit as Lose Hill Pike, but unlike the neighbouring Win Hill Pike there is no rocky outcrop here to warrant the qualification 'Pike', presumably, in this instance, it was the peak-like quality that influenced colloquial reference. The view from the topograph is dominated by the ridge largely just traversed with Mam Tor backed by Lord's Seat figuring prominently, eastward the rocky crest of Win Hill Pike catching attention.

The way down is limited to the one path leaving the summit south-eastwards, entering an old lane and passing Townhead to reach the Vale of Edale road. Go left across Townhead Bridge branching right up the lane to Fullwood Stile Farm, noting how attractively Lose Hill rises conically above the verdant pastures and trees.

The rough tracked lane heading north from Fullwood Stile has been in use at least since Roman times. Once through the gate at 800 feet the views begin to expand with the length of Edale opening up and the eastern shoulder of Kinder featuring Crookstone Knoll with Jaggers Clough running up into its flanks attracting attention ahead. The track rises steadily to Hope Cross, a restored medieval signpost, beyond which the route comes to a track junction from which there is a view south-east down to the Ladybower Reservoir marshalled by the knobbly Crook Hill and, above the plantations, Win Hill Pike (see illustration below).

Go left into Jaggers Clough, the name recalling the passage of packhorses along this stony trail. Incidentally this clough makes an excellent approach route onto Edale Moor. The clear path advances round to Rowland Cote (Edale Youth Hostel), passes infront of the buildings and on re-entering pastures contours to an access point gate, there declining through pastureland past Cotefield to enter a lane into Ollerbrook Booth. 'Oller' means 'alder' and a 'Booth' was originally a secure enclosure for domestic livestock from wild beasts such as wolves that at one time roamed the heights – note place-names like Wooler Knoll and Wove Hill, above Grindsbrook Clough.

BAMFORD EDGE

134

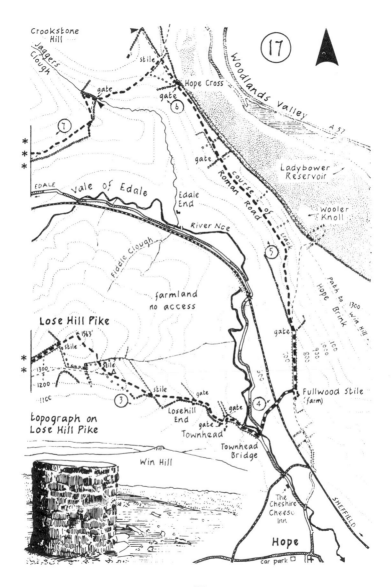

Crookstone Hill

Jaggers Clough

stile

⑰

Woodlands Valley

A 57

Hope Cross

gate

⑥

gate

⑦

* * *

gate

Course of Roman Road

Ladybower Reservoir

EDALE

Vale of Edale

Edale End

River Nce

Wooler Knoll

Fiddle Clough

⑤

track

farmland no access

Path to Win Hill

1300

Hope Brink

Lose Hill Pike

1563'

stile

* *

stile

gate

900

1100

1200

1300

stile

⑤

800

700

⑤

gate

⑥

300

Fullwood Stile (farm)

⑥

③

stile

gate

⑥

Losehill End

gate

Townhead

topograph on Lose Hill Pike

Townhead Bridge

Win Hill

The Cheshire Cheese Inn

SHEFFIELD

Hope

car park □

135

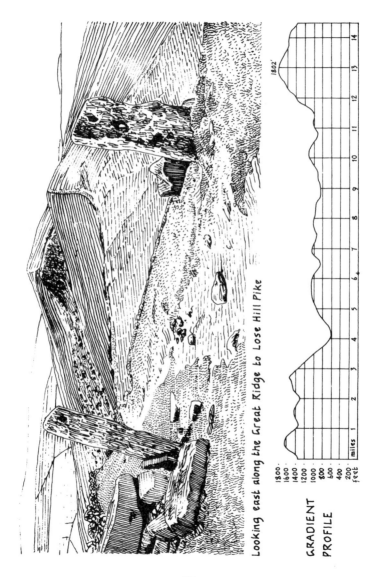

Looking east along the Great Ridge to Lose Hill Pike

GRADIENT
PROFILE

1802'

Jaggers Clough and Crookstone Knoll

Passing through the farmyard, follow the wall to a stile and across a pasture to a footbridge over Grinds Brook and proceed up the slope to pass infront of the Old Nag's Head. This fine old walkers hotel, generally deemed to be the real southern terminus of the Pennine Way, bears in its name further proof that the path you are following coincides with the old packhorse trading route.

Two popular footpath routes from Grindsbrook Booth have been included on the map to help anyone who wishes to shorten the day's proceedings. either to Hollins Cross (this path receives heavy pedestrian usage) or Mam Nick via Harden Clough.

Walkers ready and able to attack the full excursion should go forward to the gate, over the ensuing stile and up the lane to a stile on the left, following the wall left on a clear path locating a series of stiles takes the route over Broadlee Bank (notice the landslipped area here also). Descend into a lane and through the farmyard at Upper Booth, cross the road and go straight down the bank to a frail footbridge across the River Noe just by the watersmeet.

Climb the bank to another stile and cross the field, passing to the right of Highfield Farm, proceeding to Tagsnaze barn. Go through the gate, advance by two stiles to the footbridge below Dalehead (National Trust property) and go up infront of the house to the gate, turning left to reach a footbridge via a series of stiles. This little used footpath now climbs the rigg with little trace of a path especially in the upper reaches approaching the old Chapel Gate track. Go right with the old way, ignoring the short cut which has no right of way status, crossing the broad saddle of the Colborne ridge to where a lane takes the bridleway down towards Chapel-en-le-Frith. At this point go left with the ridge wall, passing the Bronze Age round barrow, associated presumably with the first incumbents of the Mam Tor fort. The barrow marks the summit of Lord's Seat, which was first recorded by this name in 1620, though the Lord's identity remains obscure.

The ridge narrowing appreciably due to the action of landslipping, conclude by the track leading diagonally off the sharp ridge to a gate below Mam Nick.

Two views from Mam Tor
(above) looking west to Lord's Seat
(below) looking north-east to Lose Hill

Marking a muleteers crossroads, Hope Cross stands on the
ridge between Win Hill and Kinder Scout - a beautiful relic

WALK 18

LANTERN PIKE
and COWN EDGE

from the Monk's Road
8 miles

When approaching Longdendale from Mottram the traveller's attention
is held by Bramah Edge and the whaleback moorland rising to Bleaklow.
However, turning into the Dinting Vale for Glossop, eyes are diverted to
Cown Edge, which appears as a peaked scarp above the town.
The first objective of this walk, Lantern Pike may seem a humble hill
but as a viewpoint it is a sheer joy, commanding a delightful prospect
of the Downfall flank of Kinder and down upon Hayfield. Overall
it is a gentle walk when measured beside outings elsewhere in the
High Peak, with easy route finding and a welcome pub at mid-course.

Mare's Back

Cown Edge Rocks

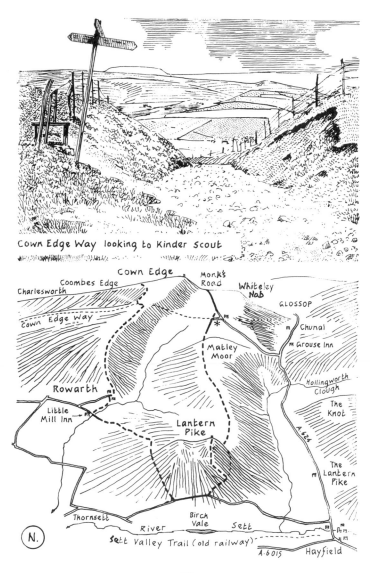

Cown Edge Way looking to Kinder Scout

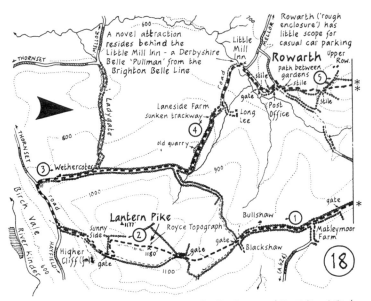

A novel attraction resides behind the Little Mill Inn - a Derbyshire Belle 'Pullman' from the Brighton Belle Line

Rowarth ('rough enclosure') has little scope for casual car parking

Rowarth
path between gardens

Little Mill Inn

Laneside Farm
sunken trackway

Long Lee

Post Office

old quarry

Wethercotes

Lantern Pike
▲1177

Royce Topograph

Bullshaw

Matleymoor Farm

Sunny Side

Blackshaw

Higher Cliff (fm)

(18)

Lantern Pike is a commanding little eminence held in the care of the National Trust to which it was given following its purchase by subscription in 1950 as a memorial to Edwin Royce — "in recognition of his labours in the cause of securing the freedom of the hills". The view indicator on the summit, where once stood a ruin resembling a castle keep (demolished in 1907) and previously flared out a warning beacon (hence the name), overlooks a steep eastern declivity with views down on Hayfield and beyond to Kinder Scout.

The Derbyshire Belle at the Little Mill Inn

142

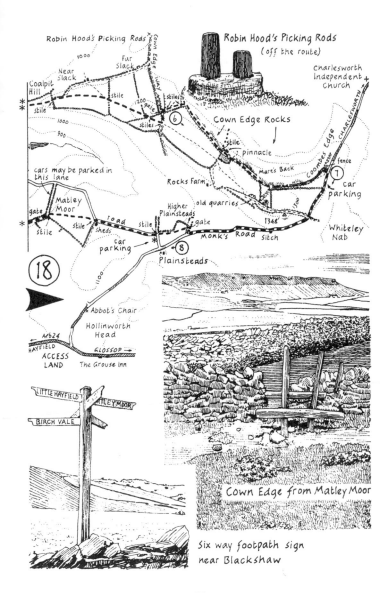

Robin Hood's Picking Rods

Robin Hood's Picking Rods
(off the route)

Near Slack

Far Slack

Coalpit Hill

10.00

stile

1200

stile

stiles

Cown Edge Way

Charlesworth Independent Church

CHARLESWORTH

Cown Edge Rocks

1000

900

stile

6

stiles

stile

pinnacle

Coombes Edge

fence

cars may be parked in this lane

Matley Moor

gate

stile

sheds

road

stile

Higher Plainsteads

Rocks Farm

Mare's Back

old quarries

7

car parking

Whiteley Nab

1358

stile

1348

gate

car parking

Monk's Road

Sitch

18

1100

8

Plainsteads

Abbot's Chair

Hollinworth Head

Nb24

HAYFIELD ACCESS LAND

GLOSSOP

The Grouse Inn

LITTLE HAYFIELD

TLEY MOOR

BIRCH VALE

Cown Edge from Matley Moor

Six way footpath sign near Blackshaw

143

The Walk :

From the lane off the Monk's Road opposite Plainsteads, proceed down the by-road signposted to Rowarth (although it is unsuitable for cars in the valley). Where the road swings right cross the stile ahead and follow a thin path through the heather of Matley Moor. Descending to a stile at the top of a walled lane, pass on through the facing gate and along the track in a southerly direction. Beyond a gate entering a lane, passing Matleymoor and Bullshaw Farms to reach a six-way signpost (see drawing), taking the footpath to Birch Vale through the gate and up the pasture to a further gate leading to a short lane. From the National Trust signboard ascend the slope with the clear path to attain the summit of Lantern Pike.

Descend with the south-trending Edge to the wall, complying with way-marks directing left down to the open track, turn right passing through the gate proceeding past Sunny Side to reach the minor road above Birch Vale. Go right, taking the first on the right past Wethercotes keeping to the sunken lane which becomes a metalled road from Laneside Farm to reach The Little Mill Inn - a popular yet secluded pub. Follow the lane leading north-east from the Inn, going through a gate avoiding the White House, to a stile onto the by-road by Rowarth Post Office.

At the junction go right then left where signposted, passing between gardens before ascending the ridge by a series of stiles. Strictly the right of way descends to Near Slack to regain the ridge by a tractor track; however, it appears to be common practice not to divert. The farmer has walled-up the ensuing gateways for stockproofing purposes, but has not impeded the footpath. Reaching the Cown Edge Way (a waymarked route) either proceed ahead on the well worn path to follow the Edge and pass the old quarry workings to descend to the Monk's Road between barbed fencing, or, preferably, go left to the small gate, with the Cown Edge Way.

The old Way is marshalled left, whilst the described route goes right over the stile, keeping close to the wall to a further fence stile. Veer right onto the Edge path to admire the enormous landslipped combe of Cown Edge Rocks, noticing the pinnacle and the grassy ridge of landslipped material known as the Mare's Back. The Edge path becomes a sunken lane descending to the Monk's Road, turn right to follow this road for one mile. Take the access lane to Higher Plainsteads, branching left through the gate descending the pasture to a wall stile to complete this most enjoyable walk.

GRADIENT
PROFILE

Lantern Pike from the south ridge

(below middle)
View east from the Royce Topograph on Lantern Pike

(bottom)
O.S. Column at the northern tip of Cown Edge

Leygatehead Moor · Ashop Edge · Sandy Heys · Kinder Downfall · KINDER SCOUT

WALK 19

CRACKEN EDGE
and SOUTH HEAD

from Chinley

7½ miles

Chinley, a name derived from Old English and meaning 'clearing in the deep valley', has long been used as a springboard for walks onto the High Peak moors because of its railway service. Trains regularly run from Manchester to Sheffield via Edale making practical expeditions linking Chinley with Kinder Scout and the Vale of Edale.

N.B. Manchester - Sheffield express trains stop at New Mills Central where the 'stopping trains' (to Sheffield) servicing this walk, can be boarded - this service is not as frequent as the express service.

CHINLEY CHURN

CRACKEN EDGE

THE NAZE

Chinley

View north from Eccles Pike

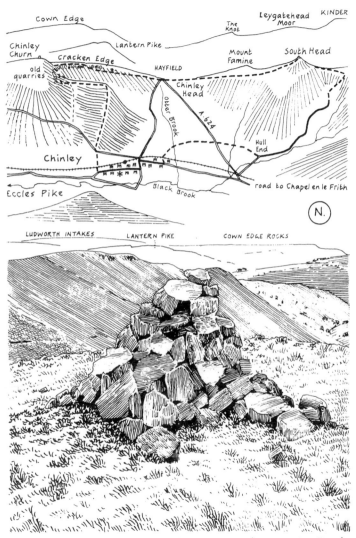

View north west over the Mount Famine ridge from South Head

The Walk:

From the car park beside the Chinley Centre go left along the Buxworth road crossing the railway footbridge and ascending the path to Stubbins Lane. Advance uphill branching into the high walled rough surfaced lane right. The lane climbs close to the Edge rising with improving views to The Naze swinging west to confront the extensive debris from Cracken Edge Quarry. The path forks, with the path right climbing diagonally above the rusting lifting gear and across a shifting slope (none too safe), the path left being preferred. Contour to a stile and as the path begins to descend (towards the upper part of Stubbins Lane) diverge upon the steeply rising path, passing a cave (see drawing) and again cross the fence, scrambling up the rocky breach beside the fence to the old quarry rim.

The O.S. column on Chinley Churn is now quite close, but be warned-this summit is strictly out-of-bounds for walkers. The name 'Churn', curiously, was coined from a rather far fetched likeness of the hill to a milk churn. The Cracken Edge Quarries, long disused and gently clothed by nature were obviously the scene of prolonged activity an impressive monument to the labours of a hardy breed of men. The quarry rim provides marvellously broad views, south to Shining Tor and Black Edge and east to South Head and Kinderlow End.

South Head from The Naze

The route slips down to follow the level grass track leading beneath the quarry face, crossing two stiles before descending across pastureland to the Hills Farm access track that sets the walker onto the minor road at Hills House. Go forward to the junction with the A.624, turning left then branch right up the lane. Turn right again at the lane junction to reach an access point gate. Follow the track diverging right to attain the summit of South Head (southern head of the Sett Valley) marked by a neat cairn.

Seen from the Sett Valley, South Head is an exciting peak, the perfect culmination to the Mount Famine ridge, but as the drawing above confirms it is not a conical summit, being more analogous with an upturned boat. Its real merits are as a viewpoint, for though Kinder End shields Kinder Downfall from sight, elsewhere there is much to admire.

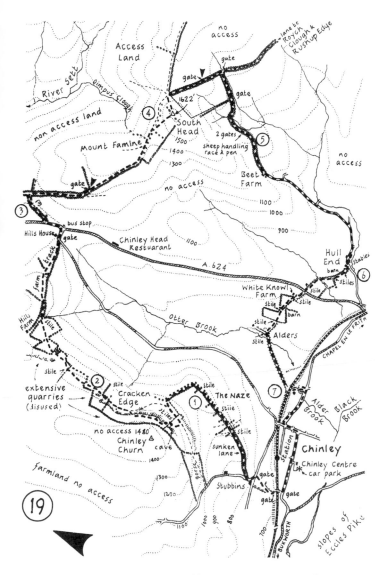

Access Land

no access

lane to Roych Clough & Rushup Edge

River Sett

Oompus Clough

gate

gate

non access land

gate

1622'

South Head

④

Mount Famine

1500

1400

1300

2 gates

sheep handling race & pen

⑤

Beet Farm

no access

no access

1100

1000

900

gate

③

bus stop

Hills House

gate

Chinley Head Restuarant

1100

A 624

Hull End

barn

stables

⑥

stile

farm track

White Knowl Farm

stiles

stile

Hills Farm

stile

Otter Brook

stile

barn

stile

Alders

CHAPEL EN LE FRITH

stile

extensive quarries (disused)

②

stile

Cracken Edge

stile

stile

①

The Naze

stile

⑦

stile

Alder Brook

Black Brook

no access 1480

Chinley Churn

cave

1400

sunken lane

station

Chinley

Chinley Centre car park

1300

1200

gate

Stubbins

gate

gate

farmland no access

⑲

1100

1600

900

800

700

BUXWORTH

slopes of Eccles Pike

149

South Head from the Sett Valley

Descend in a north easterly direction to regain the track where it enters a lane, proceeding to the lane junction, there turning right to follow the side lane down to Beet Farm. Henceforward the lane is metalled; descend to Hull End (hill end) and immediately after the stables follow the track, right, infront of the barn, following the wall to cross the A.624. Go directly over, along the access drive to White Knoll Farm passed which locate the wall stile, before descending with the wall to a further wall stile. Cross the ensuing pasture to a fence stile (the following pasture is inclined to be wet and muddy, particularly beside Alders, where the footpath joins the fenced track). Crossing Otter Brook, which rather oddly changes its name to Alder Brook to enter Chinley. Pass under the railway embankment to re-enter Chinley going right to end the day - by car or train.

South Head from Breck Edge

feet
1600
1400
1200
1000
800
600
400
200

miles 1 2 3 4 5 6 7

1622'

GRADIENT
PROFILE

Quarrying and tunnelling on Cracken Edge

Chapter Five

Divided from the Low Peak by the long Axe Edge/Morridge ridge the complicated north/south corrugations of the western moorlands present a fruitful area for the explorer on foot. Whether you seek proud summits and crags or scenes of sylvan beauty, from Hen Cloud to the Dane, or Windgather to the Dale o'Goyt there is indeed much to see and savour. This is gritstone country with a difference, rolling hills and small scattered communities, complying little to the austere hues of Bleaklow or Black Hill. A landscape of broad recreational appeal, the perfect antidote to Cheshire Plain fever!

Windgather Rocks

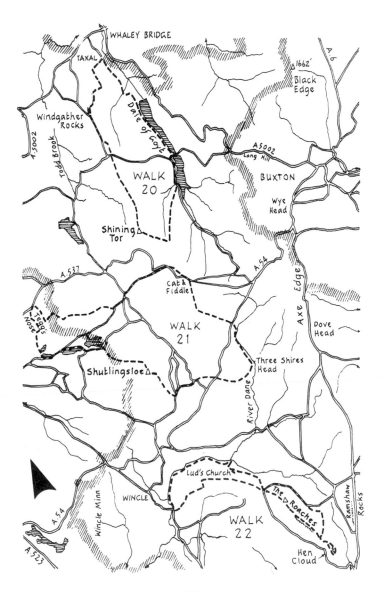

WHALEY BRIDGE

A.6

TAXAL

△ 1662'

Black
Edge

Windgather
Rocks

A.5002

Todd Brook

Dale of Goyt

A.5002
Long Hill

BUXTON

WALK
20

Wye
Head

Shining △
Tor

A.537

A.54

Axe Edge

Cat &
Fiddle

Tegg's
Nose

WALK
21

Dove
Head

Shutlingsloe △

Three Shires
Head

River Dane

A.54

Lud's Church

The △ Roaches

WINCLE

Wincle Minn

WALK
22

Ramshaw
Rocks

A.54

A.523

Hen
Cloud

WALK 20   SHINING TOR and the DALE of GOYT

from Taxal

10½ miles

This walk, part ridge, part valley, is of simple design but because objectives are well hidden and quite distant the walker is carried along by a healthy curiosity.   Few will be disappointed with Windgather Rocks, a delightful gritstone outcrop of imposing proportions.   The moorland ridge to Shining Tor may be tamer stuff but has historic connections.   The ridge path coincides with the ancient Macclesfield Forest Ridgeway. Oldgate Nick, a pass on a salt trading route where one may imagine pack-mules ladened with salt from Nantwich climbing out of the Todd valley and going in the reverse direction mule trains with bulky panniers of woollen goods.   Cats Tor points to the survival in folk memory, and therefore recorded on the earliest Ordnance map of 1840, of wild cats, that apparently found refuge upon these hills.   There is little about Shining Tor that can be said to shine from any angle, though the small outcrop of rocks just below the summit may glisten after rain.

The route retires into the beautifully wooded Dale of Goyt to track down the shores of the two reservoirs and finally by field paths to Taxal, a sequestered little community pleasantly removed from the calamitous mainstream of business and holiday activity.

Windgather Rocks

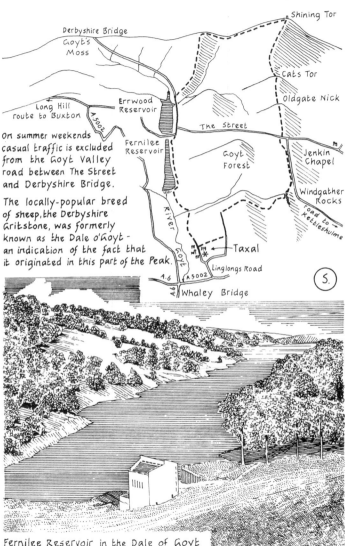

Shining Tor

Derbyshire Bridge

Goyt's Moss

Cats Tor

Oldgate Nick

Long Hill route to Buxton

A.5002

Errwood Reservoir

The Street

Jenkin Chapel

Fernilee Reservoir

Goyt Forest

On summer weekends casual traffic is excluded from the Goyt Valley road between The Street and Derbyshire Bridge.

Windgather Rocks

road to Kettleshulme

The locally-popular breed of sheep, the Derbyshire Gritstone, was formerly known as the Dale o'Goyt – an indication of the fact that it originated in this part of the Peak.

River Goyt

Taxal

Linglongs Road

(S.)

A.6   A.5002

A.6   Whaley Bridge

Fernilee Reservoir in the Dale of Goyt

155

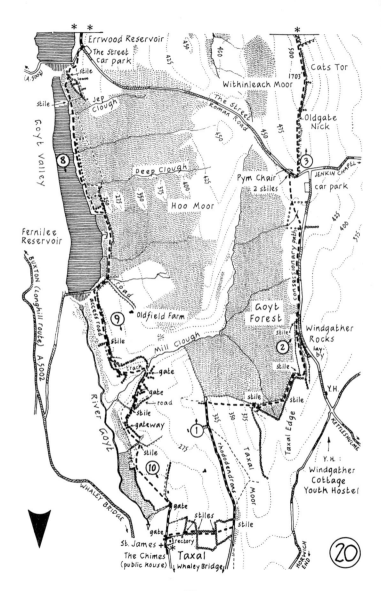

Errwood Reservoir

The Street
car park

* *

(A.5004)

stile

Jep
Clough

stile

Goyt Valley

8

Deep Clough

Fernilee
Reservoir

275

350

400

Hoo Moor

425

275

road

access road

9

Oldfield Farm

stile

track

Mill Clough

gate

gate

road

stile

gateway

stile

1

275

BUXTON (Longhill route) A.5002

River Goyt

10

WHALEY BRIDGE

gate

gate

stiles

rectory

St. James

The Chimes
(public house)

Taxal

Whaley Bridge

Withinleach Moor

450

400

425

Cats Tor

1703'

500

The Street
Roman Road

450

Oldgate
Nick

475

3

JENKIN CHAPEL

Pym Chair
2 stiles

car park

425

400

375

Goyt
Forest

stile

Windgather
Rocks

2

lay-by

stile

stile

stile

Y.H.

KETTLESHULME

Taxal Edge

Taxal Moor

rhododendrons

375

350

375

Y.H.
Windgather
Cottage
Youth Hostel

HORWICH END

20

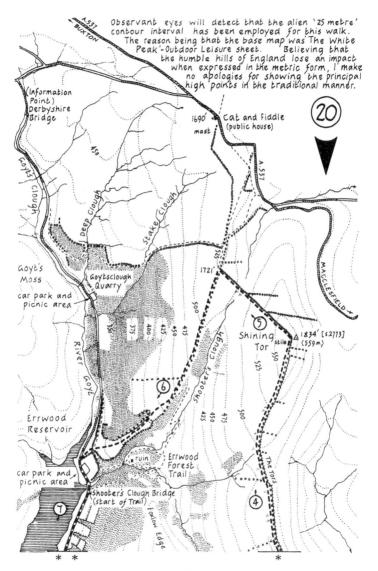

Observant eyes will detect that the alien '25 metre' contour interval has been employed for this walk. The reason being that the base map was The White Peak'- Outdoor Leisure sheet. Believing that the humble hills of England lose an impact when expressed in the metric form, I make no apologies for showing the principal high points in the traditional manner.

A.537 BUXTON

(Information Point)
Derbyshire Bridge

1690' Cat and Fiddle (public house)
mast

⑳

A.537

Goyt's Clough

Deep Clough

Stake Clough

Goyt's Moss

Goytsclough Quarry

car park and picnic area

575

1721'

500

MACCLESFIELD

⑤

Shining Tor   stile △ 1834' [s.2773]
(559m)

525

550

375 400 425 475

River Goyt

450 475 500

⑥

425 475 500

Errwood Reservoir

ruin   Errwood Forest Trail

The Tors

car park and picnic area

Shooter's Clough Bridge (start of Trail)

⑦

④

Foxlow Edge

* *   *

157

The Walk:

Reach Taxal from Horwich End via Linglongs Road. A parking area opposite the church makes a good base for this circular walk. Follow the road past the church and enter the field right beyond the Rectory, a footpath leads up the pastures to a minor road there turn left. Just short of the roadend branch right up a thin path to the ridge top nick. Pause and admire the prospect ahead, the crest of Windgather Rocks draws the eyes beyond the dark textured middleground of the Goyt Forest conifers.

Descend to the ladder stile close by the wood and follow the fence closely to enter the Windgather enclosure. Windgather Rocks are a prominent landmark, and a popular climbing ground, but their virtues as a viewpoint are no less remarkable. Walk along the edge sampling the airy blast that is suggested by the name Windgather.

Continue above the rocks proceeding to the end of the gritstone outcrop, cross the new stile and follow the newly created concessionary path alongside the road wall, inside the Forestry Commission enclosure, to join up with the footpath crossing rough pasture to two ladder stiles, onto The Street (Roman Road). Turn right to the former site of Pym Chair where a signpost directs up the ridge towards Cats and Shining Tors, the ridge path keeping the wall (boundary between Derbyshire and Cheshire) on the right. The first pronounced rise in the ridge is succeeded by Oldgate Nick: there isn't even a footpath crossing, but it is recognisable as a holloway. Here crossed a saltway from Cheshire rising from Saltersford Hall in the upper Todd valley en route for Chesterfield. Coincidently, our route from Windgather to Shining Tor follows part of the Macclesfield Forest Ridgeway, a way of great antiquity.

A wet and undistinguished path continues to the top of Shining Tor: access to the O.S. column is over a ladder stile (heed notice affixed). The view, though not so well appointed as Windgather, still has merit, with the gracious cone of Shutlingsloe, presiding over the Wildboarclough and Macclesfield Forest localities. A word of warning to walkers accustomed to the infallibility of Ordnance Survey maps: the Outdoor Leisure map clearly shows the way S.E. on the south side of the wall as from the triangulation column. This is incorrect and anyone visiting the summit must return over the ladder stile to proceed. Keep beside the wall, to its junction with the path from the Cat and Fiddle Inn, an oft used way.

Turn left down the track veering away from the wall at the sign associated with the Errwood Hall Forest Trail. Descend the pastures more steeply to cross a wall eventually reaching the

Goyt Valley road at the head of Errwood Reservoir. The immensely prudent Goyt Valley Scheme, instituted to salvage this beautiful valley from vehicular annihilation, has brought a relaxed air to this sequestered place. One may stroll along the shoreline road or delve into the rhododendron fringed environs on the Errwood Hall Forest Trail, in some peace - a relative statement with homo sapiens frequently so evident.

Deep beneath the dark waters of Errwood Reservoir languishes Goyt's Bridge where once crossed The Street, a conjectured westward extension of the Derby to Buxton Road way. Where The Street draws the lakeside road away, briefly follow the the dam road, branching left then right down the pasture to a stile, thereafter descending through the woods to the cinder track beside Fernilee Reservoir. Proceed to Deep Clough, where either ascend or continue on a narrower path until forced up to the lane by a ravine. Cross a stile onto the Oldfield Farm lane turning right to the Fernilee dam, now follow the access road which becomes an unsurfaced track leading round and down to the stoutly rustic Mill Clough Bridge. The track rises to a sharp elbow, whereupon continue to a stile following the wall to a gateway, then crossing the succeeding pasture to a stile by a small stream. The final pasture is crossed on a curving line to reach a tarmac access road passing through a gate to return to Taxal (Tātuc's nook or valley) and The Chimes for refreshment!

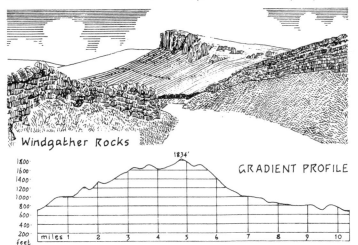

Windgather Rocks

GRADIENT PROFILE

WALK 21   SHUTLINGSLOE

from the Tegg's Nose Country Park

13½ miles

This walk contains a great diversity of scenery combined with several quite impressive viewpoints. Shutlingsloe, the graceful queen of the western moors may be the prime objective, yet the walk contrives to reveal a string of lovely and contrasting scenes and tranquil passages away from the tourist jostlings liable to be encountered at Tegg's Nose. Even as you slip into your boots in the car park, your attention is readily drawn to Shutlingsloe, rising above the dark massed conifers of Macclesfield Forest, as illustrated below.

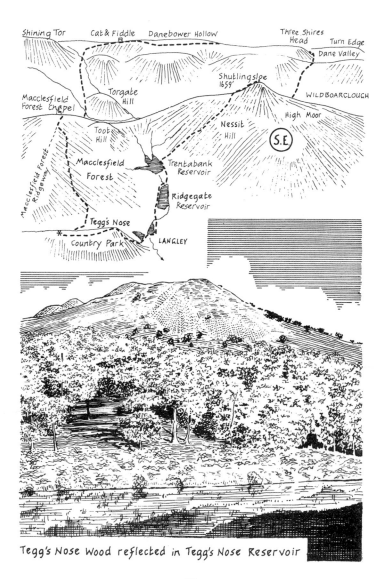

Tegg's Nose Wood reflected in Tegg's Nose Reservoir

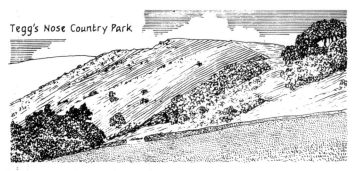

Tegg's Nose Country Park

The Walk :

From the Country Park Information Centre turn left to follow the waymarked path into the Country Park. The Centre is situated beside the Buxton Old Road (the earliest turnpike across the moors from Macclesfield)-notice the London milestone. Keep to the path by the wall pass through three kissing gates, whereupon veer sharp left with the fence to a stile, here entering the Country Park proper. Proceed past the quarry face and the restored crushing gear last used over twenty years ago. The prominent Tegg's Nose spur has been transformed with much imagination into a marvellous promenade, nature in reclaiming her hold having tempered the worst effects of dereliction and the gaping wounds of the years of stone extraction.

At the prow, just below the quarry track, stands an ingenious photographic topograph which provides an interesting survey of the valley and hill features crowding round this southward prospect. Return to the track, continuing to a stile on the left which puts the walker onto a rapidly descending path through Teggsnose Wood to a kissing gate. Cross the two impounding dams, joining the Langley road opposite a row of cottages. Follow the road left, taking the right fork at the road junction opposite The Smithy (public house). Pass Ridgegate Reservoir and fork left at the next road junction, then just after the entrance gates to Trentabank Reservoir seek a stile with a signpost directing up into the plantations right. The footpath is initially overwhelmed by a claustrophobic canopy of conifers - spelling a death to ground flora and fauna - mercifully the constriction relents somewhat on the rise under Nessit Hill. Nevertheless, this stile onto High Moor comes as a considerable relief, from where a well defined path ascends the heather moor to the ridgetop fence stile. Go right with the wall to a stile in the corner; ahead, the first goal of the expedition, is only a short stiff climb away. Shutlingsloe, which means 'Scyttel's hill', has only recently become accessible as the path running over the summit was only made a legal right of way in 1980.

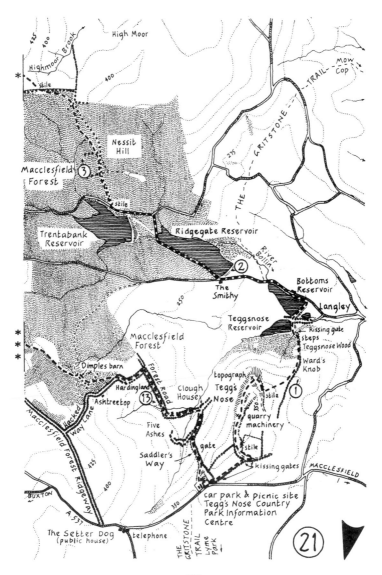

High Moor

Highmoor Brook

* stile

Nessit Hill

Macclesfield Forest ③

stile

Trentabank Reservoir

Ridgegate Reservoir

River Bollin

②

The Smithy

Bottoms Reservoir

Langley

Teggsnose Reservoir

Kissing gate
steps
Teggsnose Wood

Macclesfield Forest

Ward's Knob

Dimples barn

topograph

*
*
*

Hardingland

Clough House

Tegg's Nose

stile

①

Ashtreetop

⑬

quarry machinery

Five Ashes

gate

stile

Saddler's Way

kissing gates

MACCLESFIELD

Macclesfield Forest Ridgeway

Hacked Way Lane

BUXTON

A 537

car park & picnic site
Tegg's Nose Country
Park Information
Centre

The Setter Dog
(public house)

telephone

THE GRITSTONE TRAIL Lyme Park

THE GRITSTONE TRAIL

Mow Cop

②①

View north from Shutlingsloe

Shutlingsloe soars gracefully to dominate the western moors, its summit is in the best tradition of mountain tops, a rocky crest above a steep eastern declivity giving tremendous airy spaciousness to the view. The eastern arc includes The Roaches (see illustration) and Ramshaw Rocks backed by Morridge with Taggsclough Hill closer to hand. Prominent among the trees of Wildboarclough, stands Crag Hall with the old mill pond below. Above rise Cut-thorn Hill and Turn Edge about Three Shires Head, beyond rises Oliver Hill and peeping above the skyline by Flash is Sheen Hill in the Dove valley. Above the wooded Cumberland Brook is Dane Bower Hill and the Whetstone Ridge backed by Axe Edge Moor, due east. Next comes the Cat and Fiddle Inn identified by a mast, to its left is Goyt's Moss leading into the scene depicted above. From Bow Stones the western arc of the view commences with Sponds Hill above the plantations of Macclesfield Forest. Tegg's Nose is clearly seen with the recently passed plantation upon Nessit Hill in the foreground. The town of Macclesfield leads the eye across the broad Cheshire Plain to the sandstone ridge of Delamere Forest backed by the Clwydian Hills. Keen eyes may isolate Jodrell Bank Radio Telescope due west, whilst the white dishes may not be apparent to all visitors the transmitter on Sutton Common most certainly will be. Beyond Wincle Minn can be seen The Cloud and Mow Cop, southwards rises Gun above Tittesworth Reservoir with the Back Forest ridge above the River Dane linking to The Roaches to complete the panorama.

The Roaches from Shutlingsloe

Crag Mill, Wildboarclough

Descend the steep eastern flank of the hill to join the metalled farm access road that crosses a cattle grid and proceeds to meet the valley road. Understandably, there will be a great temptation to patronise the Crag Inn (as did the author), but don't overdo it as there is still some way to go! The route goes left then right over the Clough Brook bridge going up the road past the former Crag Mill administrative building which for a time served as a sub-post office of somewhat generous proportions. Proceeding by the delightful parish church, the route passes Crag Hall continuing uphill from the junction, branch up the lane where the road swings right and from the gate advance across pastureland to a stile onto the A.54.

From the opposing stile follow the ditch to a wall gap across the watershed, continuing to a stile close to Cut-thorn Cottage. Cross the minor road to join the rough track leading to the Three Shire (Shires) Heads (Head) watersmeet, enjoying in the process the pleasant Dane valley scene, enhanced as it is by The Roaches ridge. The confluence, known to this day as Panniers Pool, must have been an important bifurcation in the passage of packhorse tradesmen. The name Three Shire Heads (O.S. maps) seems out of step with vernacular since taken literally it implies that three shire horses were decapitated or that sheriffs met here from the three counties to discuss, duel or resolve matters of mutal concern - my map complies with the simple truth of the name, which means the point where the three counties of Staffordshire, Derbyshire and Cheshire coincide.

Continuing upon the track beside the River Dane, where the track rises with a wall cross the pasture to a stile, keeping straight to a fixed gate beside the stream. Climb over and proceed close to the stream till the path rises gently away from the stream beyond the fence-end. Attaining a wall stile climb diagonally more steeply, passing under the mine air shaft to join a track. Go immediately left through the gate continuing to the A.57 again. Go right with the main road to a stile on the left, at the brow of the hill. The route advances with the man-made boundary dike (linear grough!) known as Danebower Hollow which leads via a gate onto a track to the Cat&Fiddle.

48 miles   2¼ miles   13miles   8 miles
The Wrekin   Shutlingsloe   Mow Cop   The Cloud

A.537

View south from the old road

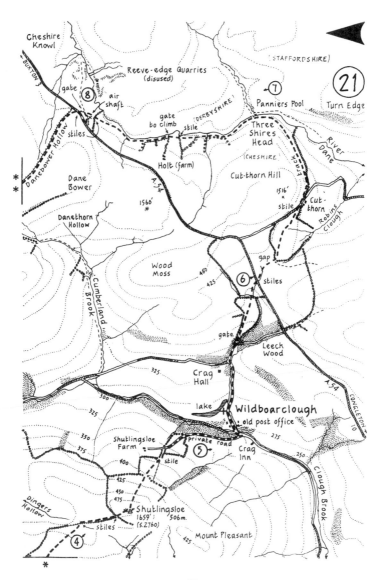

The name Cat and Fiddle is said to have been coined by the landlord in 1857 when the Duke of Devonshire gave him a photograph of a cat playing a violin presumably like the delightful sculpted relief on the porch. With memories of the long haul from Trentabank onto Shutlingsloe it may be galling to realise that motorists calling in here for a casual drink are doing so a full thirty one feet higher than the walker with his flask upon that peak!

From the Inn follow the A.537 joining the cobbled track, which is the original surface of the 1759 turnpike road. Opposite the Shining Tor Restaurant cross the main road and descend the minor road (continuation of the first turnpike). This unfortunate and unavoidable road tramp passes Torgate Farm (a possible reference to the ancient Macclesfield Forest Ridgeway that apparently slipped down from Shining Tor and passed this way), en route for the third public house on the walk so far (verging on a pub crawl!), the Stanley Arms. At the road junction turn left, taking the right fork at the next junction and then branching right again into Oven-House Lane (hence 'Bottom-of-the-Oven'). Presumably a communal bread oven (bakehouse) at one time existed in this lane, which rises to pass into the charming little community of Macclesfield Forest set just beyond St. Stephen's Chapel where the traditional custom of rush-bearing is still observed each year on the nearest Sunday to the 12th August.

Take the lane leading right up the ridge, seeking the footpath diverging left at the beginning of the forestry. A clearly marked path delves through the trees with the occasional respite to reach the derelict and curiously named barn called simply 'Dimples'! The route passes below the barn, veering left at a path fork to leave the trees into Hacked Way Lane. Pass Hardingland and follow Forest Road (a narrow lane) down to Clough House, where turn right up the Saddler's Way lane to the Country Park Centre car park.

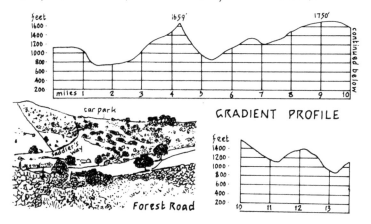

GRADIENT PROFILE

Forest Road

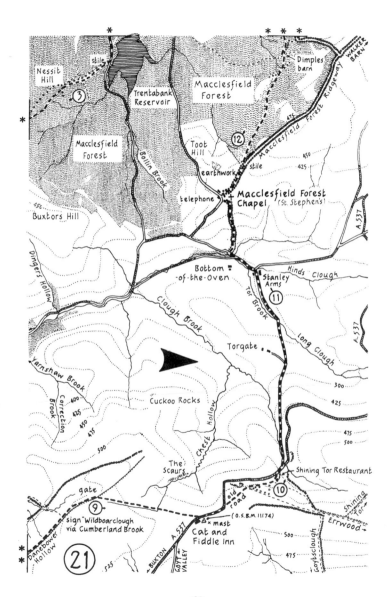

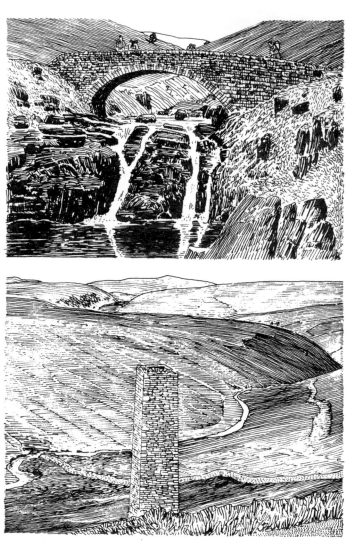

(above) Pannier's Pool Bridge   (below) Upper Dane Valley

Macclesfield Forest Chapel

Plaque on the porch of The Cat and Fiddle Inn

THE CAT & FIDDLE

WALK 22

from Danebridge

THE ROACHES

11¼ miles

The village of Wincle nestles in the dell of the River Dane from where the proximity of great rocks and wild moors is little suspected. Yet all approaches to this spot give some warning of the bold swell of The Roaches and the dramatic impact they have on an otherwise rolling landscape cannot be denied. To feel the rocks under your boots, with the wall of Roaches Grit (illustration above) as a promenade or to stand beneath the sheer walls at the southern end of the outcrop and there gasp at the flamboyant style and courage of rock climbers (see facing illustration) are but two of the exceptional pleasures of this excursion.

The name 'Roaches' is almost pure French, deriving from 'Roche' meaning 'rock', no more description being necessary. Geologically they belong to the Goyt Syncline which runs south through Ramshaw Rocks then suddenly diverts sharp north on the Hen Cloud. The outcrop rises in an inverted 'V' presenting what may be considered to be the first bastions of Highland Britain facing south to the softer landscapes of Midland England. Successive layers of grit, mudstone and sandstone folding down beneath the coal bearing basin of Goldsitch Moss about the headwaters of Black Brook, plunging at 40° north from Hen Cloud.

The walk described differs from the general pattern within this guide in that it is almost a figure-of-eight, thus offering alternative starting points together with options on circuit lengths to suit your time and energy.

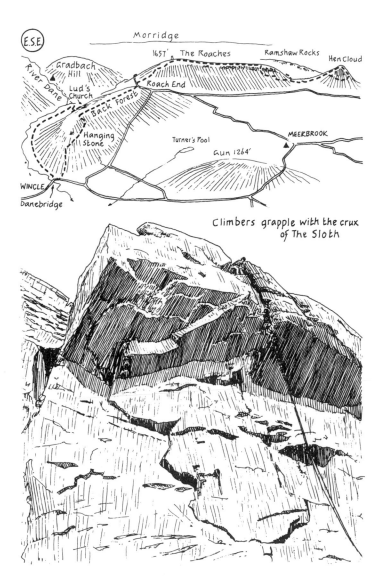

E.S.E.

Morridge

Gradbach Hill

River Dane

Lud's Church

Back Forest

Hanging Stone

1657' The Roaches

Ramshaw Rocks

Hen Cloud

Roach End

Turner's Pool

MEERBROOK

Gun 1264'

WINCLE

Danebridge

Climbers grapple with the crux of The Sloth

The Walk :

From Danebridge, where there is limited roadside parking, follow the road south for 100 yards to a footpath sign pointing up beside the houses left. Ascend the steps and pass through the narrow hedged passage to a stile, then follow the fence on the left to a stile into the wood, soon to join a broad path that comes up from Danebridge (not a right of way). Descend briefly to cross a stream climb to a stile out of the wood and cross the pasture to Hangingstone Farm (notice the Hangingstone Rock on the hillside beyond the farm). Pass through the farmyard to the left of the farmhouse. Mount the tapered enclosure to a small gate onto the contouring track that now leads the route under the enormous projecting cannon, hanging in space before the slope, hence the name Hanging Stone. A lane enters from the right taking the route to Paddock (house); go forward to a gate, noting the helpful warning affixed regarding the timidity of Highland cattle at pasture in the succeeding field — always walk slowly round them From the next stile turn up the track left, where a sunken way crosses the Back Forest ridge. Where the open moor is reached branch right off the old track onto the signposted concessionary ridge path. This path holds to the ridge crest mounting several outcrops and proceeding to a stile onto the Roach End road.

There is some scope for car parking here and as the walk returns to this point from Hen Cloud then it may well be used as an alternative starting point.

A well used path mounts through the heather, the O.S. accredit the name Bearstone Rock to some insignificant boulders, the name would be more appropriately applied to the rocks flanking the path nearer the summit (see illustration). The summit of The Roaches is marked by an Ordnance Survey column and walkers will no doubt halt awhile to enjoy the fine prospect with Shutlingsloe prominent to the north-west, rising a mere two feet higher at 1659'.

Wind weathered gritstone outcrops

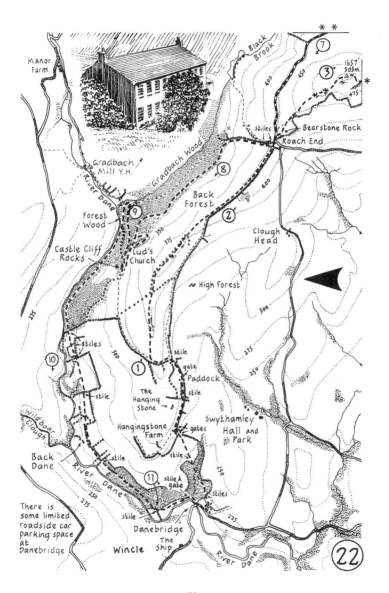

Manor Farm

Black Brook

* *

⑦

450

400

1657 505m. ③ △ *

475

stiles

Bearstone Rock

Roach End

Gradbach Mill Y.H.

River Dane

Gradbach Wood

⑧

Back Forest

400

②

Forest Wood

⑨

350

375

Clough Head

Castle Cliff Rocks

Lud's Church

~ High Forest

300

225

300

275

stiles

stile

⑩

stile

①

gate

Paddock

250

The Hanging Stone

stile

stile

250

Swythamley Hall and Park

Wildboar Clough

Hangingstone Farm

gates

300

Back Dane

River Dane

stile

stile

250

250

⑪

stile & gate

stiles

225

250

There is some limited roadside car parking space at Danebridge

275

stile

Danebridge

Wincle

The Ship

River Dane

㉒

175

The ridge path now begins the gradual southern descent and though the views so far have been enjoyable, real thrills lie in store, for soon the path reaches the craggy rim. Cross the broken wall then follow it down by Doxey Pool. Here a small patch of muddy peat overlying the sandstone has impeded the normal free drainage to form a shallow basin pond. Interestingly Doxey is recorded in the Domesday Book as Dochesig and appears to derive from personal name 'Docc' which is not evidenced elsewhere.

Doxey Pool

The Edge path descends to a natural break in the otherwise continuous outcrop. There slip down the gully veering left where the fence ends to traverse under the magnificent sheer walls of the Upper Tier. This Gargantuan uplift is riven along lines of weakness into giant slabs divided by cracks, chimneys and overhanging pinnacles - a challenge no red blooded rock-climber could resist. The most imposing buttress occurs near the southern end of the principal outcrop (see illustration at the beginning of the walk), an intimidating overhang capping the high wall has a narrow crack leading to the top of the crag. Any climber who leads The Sloth must have a cool head and strong hands. The route now seeks the Rockhall Steps which lead down the Lower Tier to pass Rockhall Cottage. quaint dwelling hugging the cliff, formerly a gamekeepers house, it has lately been the abode of 'Doug, Lord of the Roches' who has craved the attention of passers-by with unsubtle comments in red paint. The route keeps with the track beneath the cottage enclosure (notice the steps cut into the huge boulder) then turns left at the wall.

The inclusion of Hen Cloud (which means 'high rock' not 'fowl mist'!) is optional, but for such little extra effort you may enjoy a superb view and claim a real peak, which is indeed a rarity in High Peak.

Leave the track at the stile, cross the ensuing pasture to a further stile and ascend the obvious ridge path to attain the summit rocks and no doubt reach into your pack for a well earned snack. A climbers' path slips down beneath the crags, but the prime walkers path continues south enjoying in the process the impressive view north-east of the serrated Ramshaw Rocks edge. The path runs steeply into light woodland, there swinging right to join the access track from The Roaches House. Watch carefully for the narrow trod that contours across the steep western flank of Hen Cloud, well below the crags which undulates latterly round to the path ascended earlier.

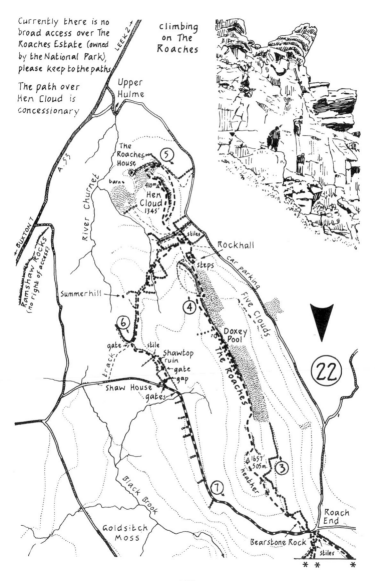

Currently there is no broad access over The Roaches Estate (owned by the National Park), please keep to the paths

The path over Hen Cloud is concessionary

climbing on The Roaches

LEEK 2¼

Upper Hulme

A 53

The Roaches House

barn

410m Hen Cloud 1345'

River Churnet

BURTON 7

Ramshaw Rocks (no right of access)

⑤

stiles

Rockhall

steps

car parking

Summerhill

④

Five Clouds

Doxey Pool

⑥

gate

stile

Shawtop ruin

gate gap

The Roaches

track

Shaw House gates

▲ 1657 505m

③

heather

Black Brook

⑦

Goldsitch Moss

Roach End

Bearstone Rock

stiles

* * *

▲ 22

177

After the stile from Hen Cloud, follow the track east, bearing north by a wall. Cross the headwaters of the River Churnet, which incidently is an old British river-name, eventually joining an access track from Summerhill. The track leads to a gate, veer sharp left, leaving the track, to follow the fence closely to a stile proceeding past the sad ruin of Shawtop by two gates onto the minor road by Shaw House. There is a beautiful feeling of spaciousness to the moorland landscape hereabouts, the name 'shaw' coming from the Old English 'scaga' meaning 'copse' evidence that considerable woodland has been lost from the locality. Down the slope from Shaw House a line of shafts mark part of the Goldsitch Moss coal mine, a fuel source predominantly for the once thriving lime-burning industry.

Follow the minor road left, going through the gate; this is a popular byway beloved by motorists but no less pleasant for walkers. The road descends to Roach End again, where leave the road with the track right, watch for the stile newly sited in the wall on the left. A clear path follows the wall down to the upper fringe of Forest Wood, the main waymarked path continuing into the woodland to the bridge to Gradbach (a point reached in due course by the described walk). However, branch left abiding to the contouring path above the steep declivity (not waymarked). After half a mile there is an obvious deviation to the left which leads by light woodland into the upper end of the Lud's Church rift. Preferably bear right keeping the minor rift depression to the right, soon passing a narrow side entrance into Lud's Church. Delve within, it's a fascinating place of quite remarkable proportions. This unique chasm, a mysterious and enveloping place where one may imagine spirits lurk, was created by a freak splitting of the hillside.
The name is attributed to Walter de Ludank, a follower of Wiclif who is said to have held secret services here in the 14th C., hence 'church'.

It is easy to see how legendary deeds or meetings could be associated with this spot, which must have figured in local life as a place of reverence, a sanctuary for many years past. Venture from these intimate walls to join the track by Castle Cliff Rocks, a fine viewpoint out of the woods into the Dane valley. Turn right, down to the signpost just short of the Gradbach footbridge (where Youth Hostellers will join the walk). Branch left keeping to the clear path through woodland above and beside the chattering merry waters of the River Dane, an old British river-name related to Middle Welsh 'dafn' meaning 'a trickling stream'. On emerging from the woods watch for the rising path which goes immediately above the isolated cottage, which on my visit was the home of a litter of pigs. Just beyond Back Dane there is a brief glimpse of Shutlingsloe framed by the wooded slopes of Wildboarclough, an exquisite scene of emerald beauty.
The Dane valley path leads into the last passage of woodland and across a meadow onto a muddy lane and so to Danebridge at journey's end.
NB.
For those curious to know the name Wincle is derived from 'Wineca's hill'.

Lud's Church

Two aspects of Hen Cloud

Summit cliffs looking south

Ramshaw Rocks from Hen Cloud

Dane Valley, featuring Shutlingsloe

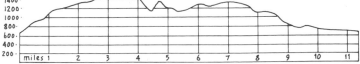

GRADIENT PROFILE

feet
1600·
1400·
1200·
1000·
800·
600·
400·
200·

1651'

miles 1   2   3   4   5   6   7   8   9   10   11

THE MARSDEN TO EDALE WALK
The Classic High Peak One Day Trek of 21 miles

It may be hard for an outsider to understand the reason for the Marsden to Edale's popularity, you either have to explore, as I have, the moorlands with a willingness to appreciate their own peculiar intrinsic beauty or live within sight of their brooding presence to know the rewards.
To meet the obvious challenge of this triple-plateau traverse becomes a compelling resolve once the initial diffidence with the terrain is overcome. The peat grough landscape can vary from a sinister threat to life to a teasing nuisance when miles have to be covered depending on the vagaries of the weather, location and physical state. If a crossing is undertaken when the sky is clear from dawn to dusk and a hard frost cements the peat, or a drought leaves all tinder dry then there is every chance that high spirits can be maintained throughout. The Pennine climate has a knack of being far meaner and the execrable perplexity of the grough drainage system may sap the resolve of any luckless soul hell-bent on journey's end.

The concept of walking from Marsden to Edale is far older than the National Park, its history is comparable with the pioneering days of rock-climbing in the Peak. Mill workers had always sought sure release from their drear existence by venturing deep into the moorland that formed a backcloth to their daily labours, but as free time expanded, inevitably, so too did walking horizons. The credit for introducing the Marsden to Edale as an expression of this adventurism has always rested upon Cecil Dawson, a Manchester cotton merchant, who, by his fleet-footed walking/running achievements helped to bring a respectability and competitive edge to bogtrotting in the early years of the present century.

The route has held its appeal, despite the proliferation of challenge walks throughout Peakland, no doubt because of the simplicity of the concept. The combination of a potentially hazardous terrain, a certain flexibility in route choice and its length being compatible with a good day out, both in summer or winter, thereby established it as a ready challenge even to seasoned bogtrotters.

Being able to fix terminal points on railway stations was the crucial factor in the success of the traverse. The walk has always been deemed to start at Marsden station, trekking against the prevailing weather, to greet the verdant beauty of the Vale of Edale as a reward for the many miles of bleak moorland consumed. The all-in-one-day traditionalist may scorn, but the route can conveniently be split into three stages for a more leisurely approach, making Marsden, Crowden and Hagg Farm Youth Hostels the staging posts, thus offering a greater degree of route choice.

Whilst the route I have adopted complies with the definition of a high-level traverse, I have not chosen to wallow in adversity.

In the early days it was not uncommon to seek the rough stuff with an almost masochistic urgency and fervour, leaping onto (into!) White Moss and bounding across Kinder Scout at full girth. Such eccentricities are no doubt still practiced, but with the welfare of new aspirants in mind, it would be imprudent to take the strenuous options. Also, I would be doing a disservice to the Park Ranger Service if the nature of the task was minimised. To cross, in one day, Black Hill, Bleaklow and Kinder Scout en bloc is certainly a formidable undertaking and some measure of physical hardship is implicit.

The Marsden to Edale captures the spirit and feel of the High Peak and can be a useful test for anyone contemplating one of the more mammouth endurance treks like the Derwent Watershed Walk.

A WESSENDEN PREAMBLE –

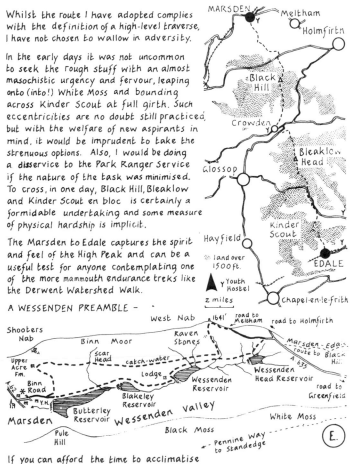

If you can afford the time to acclimatise then I recommend a gentle preliminary exercise exploring the environs of the Wessenden valley, as indicated on the diagram above and detailed on the route map over. If overnight accommodation is booked at the Marsden Youth Hostel then an afternoon stroll prior to the day of embarkation will serve to attune the mind to the task ahead. The view from West Nab of Black Hill against an evening sky is a sure enticement.

St. Bartholomew's Church, Marsden

Advancing up the Wessenden valley beside
Butterley Reservoir looking to the Blakeley dam

Pule Hill

Wessenden
Lodge

Wessenden Reservoir

The rhododendron
enveloped outflow of
Wessenden Reservoir
- an exotic alpine
garden

View south from
West Nab

Holme Edge

Black Hill

187

MELTHAM

Leyzing
Clough   sluice   aqueduct

Wessenden Moor

3

1641'
shelter West Nab

Raven
Rocks

Rocking
Stone

1500

1400

Wessenden Reservoir

1500

1100

1400

Hey
Sike

waterfall

Wessenden Lodge

Hey
Dike
Stile

2

Pennine Way

rough road

feeding Deer Hill Reservoir

Blakeley
Reservoir

stile + stream crossing

Scar
Head

Rams Clough

CALCA-water

Binn
Moor

1

Butterley
Reservoir

1200

900

Upper
Acre Farm

gates

800

Binn Road

700

700

old
Youth Hostel

slopes of
Pule Hill

Challenge
Events
commence
here

WC

bus
stop

Marsden

MELTHAM

900

B.6107

800

A.62

RIVER Colne

Huddersfield
Canal

HUDDERSFIELD

A.62

Greenhill

Station

The friendly little
township of Marsden, set
in a deep fold of the Pennine
moors, at the head of the Colne
valley seven miles from Huddersfield,
flourished as a cotton mill town.
A community has existed here over many
centuries, the name was recorded first
in 1277 as 'Marchesden', meaning
'boundary valley', though what
boundary is not clear other than Yorkshire
and Lancashire. The secretive Wessenden
valley must, too, have held a community
despite its bleak situation, allied to
the Meltham district to which it was
the 'west valley'.

The route advances out of Marsden by
Binn Road passing the old Co-op building
transformed into a most comfortable
Youth Hostel.* Keeping to the rough
lane beside the two lower reservoirs,
the route reaches Wessenden Lodge
(the last occupied house en route until
Crowden, eight inhospitable miles on),
thereon a simple path heads up the valley.
Butterley implies lush pasture
sufficient for dairy products.
Leyzing is Old Norse for 'a
freedman', an interesting survival.

* YH closed in 1983

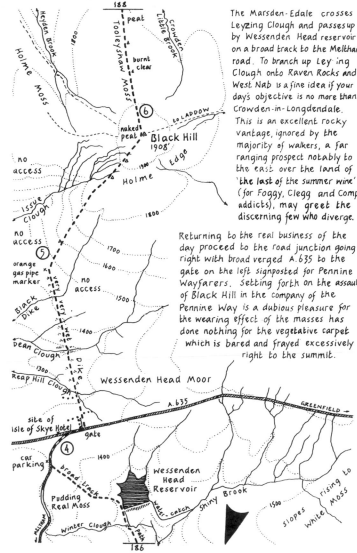

The Marsden-Edale crosses Leyzing Clough and passes up by Wessenden Head reservoir on a broad track to the Meltham road. To branch up Ley'ing Clough onto Raven Rocks and West Nab is a fine idea if your day's objective is no more than Crowden-in-Longdendale. This is an excellent rocky vantage, ignored by the majority of walkers, a far ranging prospect notably to the east over the land of 'the last of the summer wine' (for Foggy, Clegg and Compo addicts), may greet the discerning few who diverge.

Returning to the real business of the day proceed to the road junction going right with broad verged A.635 to the gate on the left signposted for Pennine Wayfarers. Setting forth on the assault of Black Hill in the company of the Pennine Way is a dubious pleasure for the wearing effect of the masses has done nothing for the vegetative carpet which is bared and frayed excessively right to the summit.

Map labels: Heyden Brook, Holme Moss, 1700, peat, Tooleyshaw Moss, 188, Crowden Little Brook, burnt clear, ⑥, to LADDOW, naked peat, Black Hill 1908', Holme Edge, 1900, no access, Issue Clough, 1800, no access, ⑤, 1700, orange gas pipe marker, 1600, no access, 1500, Black Dike, very very wet, 1400, Dean Clough, Dike, 1300, Reap Hill Clough, Wessenden Head Moor, A.635, GREENFIELD, site of Isle of Skye Hotel, gate, ④, car parking, 1400, broad track, to MELTHAM, Pudding Real Moss, Wessenden Head Reservoir, water catch, Shiny Brook, 1500, slopes rising to White Moss, Winter Clough, PW, 186

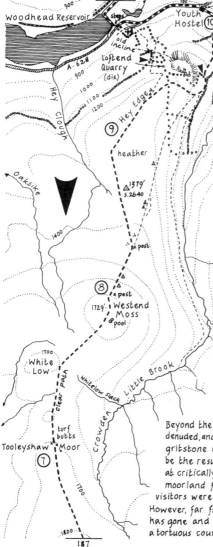

It seems odd to me that the Corps of the Royal Engineers should choose Black Hill as a suitable vantage to establish a triangulation **station**, however, in 1784 this they did, building a timber frame to mount their 36" Great Ramsden theodolite (this instrument survives and is on display at the Science Museum, Kensington). Soldiers Lump, a name subsequently given to this summit, is no viewpoint but distant features can be seen to east and west hence it has a clear survey role, though walkers need to venture onto Holme Edge to enjoy any real prospects.

Whilst the Pennine Way slips away to the s.w., our route heads s.s.e. from Black Hill along the broad featureless wilderness of Tooleyshaw Moss. Beyond the six mile point the peat is totally denuded, and this firm stretch of bedrock gritstone is a sad reminder of what can be the result when people are careless at critically dry times. Many dreadful moorland fires need never occur if all visitors were mindful of their own actions. However, far from all the high plateau peat has gone and the ridge path soon has to thread a tortuous course through the weathered hags.

Progress improves once the shoulder of Tooleyshaw Moor is reached, as wet tussocky moor replaces the raw peat down over White Low (the 'white' is a reference to the abundance of cotton-grass), and Westend Moss (the name must derive from a Heyden source, from where it holds a western aspect). The going improves still further if the popular path trending off the heather moor is adopted. However, the right of way proceeds on an intermittent path passing a trig. point set in unusually dense heather (for Black Hill that is!), and marches along Hey Edge which is quite a nice viewpoint for upper Longdendale. Speed merchants can descend from the end of the ridge down the steep slope to cross the old Loftend incline to climb the ladder stile beside Woodhead Chapel. Anyone who by accident or design opts to spend a comfortable night in Crowden Hostel, will follow the clear path round Loftend Quarry and steeply down from the access point, on a greatly scoured away path. Crowden provides a base for lightweight campers, but this is regretfully liable to winter season closure so enquire in advance if you prefer to backpack the route. Bleaklow is concealed by a wall of gritstone edges, but its looming presence will have been apparent on the long descent of Tooleyshaw and Westend Mosses, therefore, the challenge of the great landmass will already be fixed in your mind as you head up the busy A.628 (mercifully upon a pavement), rejoining the swift route below Woodhead Chapel. Descend the flight of steps and cross the Woodhead dam.

Black Hill from the frozen
fen of Westend Moss
Woodhead Chapel (right)

189

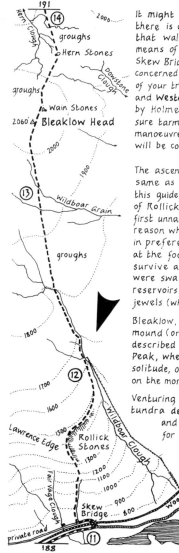

It might be worth pointing out at this stage that there is a precious safety route off Black Hill that walkers may prefer as an alternative means of reaching the foot of this ascent at Skew Bridge. If you are enveloped in mist or concerned not to lose time at this early stage of your traverse floundering over Tooleyshaw and Westend Mosses, you may profitably divert by Holme Moss to descend Heyden with the sure tarmac strip of the A.6024. This jinking manoeuvre is not possible with Bleaklow, you will be committed to the Snake or bust!

The ascent from Skew Bridge is precisely the same as that described in Walk 5, earlier in this guide. Branching up to the prominent ridge of Rollick Stones most conveniently with the first unnamed watercourse, though there is no reason why Fair Vage Clough may no be used in preference. The old (ruinous) Paper Mill at the foot of this clough is the only one to survive above Tintwistle, at least four mills were swallowed up by the string of five reservoirs that line Longdendale like sparkling jewels (when full!).

Bleaklow, which appropriately means 'the black mound (or tumulus), has been accurately described as 'the only true wilderness of the Peak, where the walker can find that real solitude, only possible in exceptional conditions on the more popular Kinder Scout!

Venturing on any traverse across this semi-tundra desert of acid peat calls for determination, and to gain meaningfully, some sympathy for the wild beauty expressed in the grotesque peatscape, where botanical life is quite literally at the end of its tether. Please heed! that Wildboar Clough is no place for non-scramblers under any conditions, or circumstances.

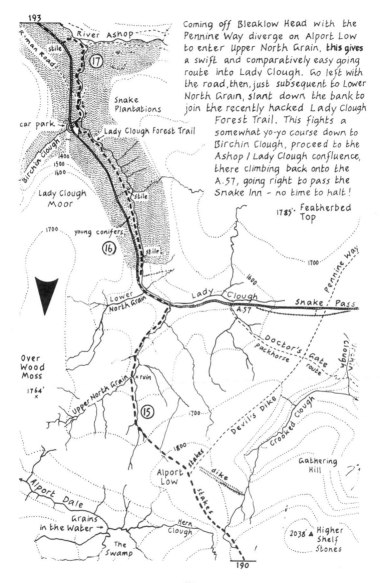

Coming off Bleaklow Head with the
Pennine Way diverge on Alport Low
to enter Upper North Grain, **this gives**
a swift and comparatively easy going
route into Lady Clough. Go left with
the road, then, just subsequent to Lower
North Grain, slant down the bank to
join the recently hacked Lady Clough
Forest Trail. This fights a
somewhat yo-yo course down to
Birchin Clough, proceed to the
Ashop / Lady Clough confluence,
there climbing back onto the
A.57, going right to pass the
Snake Inn – no time to halt!

193

River Ashop

R'man Road

stile

17

Snake
Plantations

car park

Lady Clough Forest Trail

Birchin Clough

1400
1500
1600

Lady Clough
Moor

stile

1700   young conifers

16

stile

Lower
North Grain   Lady   Clough   Snake Pass

A.57

1785'. Featherbed
Top

1700

Pennine Way

1600

Over
Wood
Moss

1764'
x

Upper North Grain   x ruin

15

1700

Doctor's Gate
Packhorse   route

Crooked Clough

Devil's Dike

Gathering
Hill

1800

stakes

Alport
Low   dike

stakes

Alport Dale

Grains
in the Water →

Hern
Clough

The
Swamp

2038 ▲ Higher
Shelf
Stones

190

The route adopted from the Snake Inn is first and foremost the safest and most direct link between the upper Woodlands valley and Grindsbrook Booth that still agrees to the definition of the Marsden to Edale walk.   However, I am aware that certain walkers would never dream of taking short measure of Kinder. It is not uncommon for experienced boghoppers to continue with the Pennine Way to the Snake Road summit, then veer over Featherbed Top into Upper Gate Clough (which might relate to the long lost Roman 'gate'), to attack Black Ashop Moor ahead of a full girth traverse of Kinder Scout. My concern has been to introduce the 'kinder' face of Kinder, whilst not denying the sporting nature of this walk - you are at liberty to follow your own inclinations, though by this stage fatigue and the advancing day are crucial factors not to be overlooked.

From the A.57, 350 yards below the Snake Inn, locate the path that slips down through the narrow belt of conifers to a footbridge across the River Ashop, a well marked path swings round to ford Fair Brook mounting the opposing slope, climbing up into Gate Side Clough (originally a cabin and grouse-shooting butts approach path).
The path disappears but your way is tangible enough, directly up with the broken wall onto Seal Stones.   The Kinder Edges path (formerly a beaters trod) is now followed left, contouring along the eroded hag fringe round Blackden Head, seeking the narrow neck of moor known, for obvious reasons, as the 'seven minute crossing'.   Do not take a compass bearing from Seal Stones to the top of Dry Clough, for a rocky ravine interposes effectively ruling out bee-lines. The 'seven minute crossing' has no path, and in mist the decision of where to diverge from the Edges path becomes a matter of faith, in clear weather the dip in the moor is quite apparent.   The declivity into Grindsbrook Clough is steep but not dangerous, excepting if weary walkers stray in mist or gathering gloom onto Nether or Upper Tors.

'seven minute crossing'

Upper Tor   Dry   Nether Tor   The Nab
         Clough

Edale

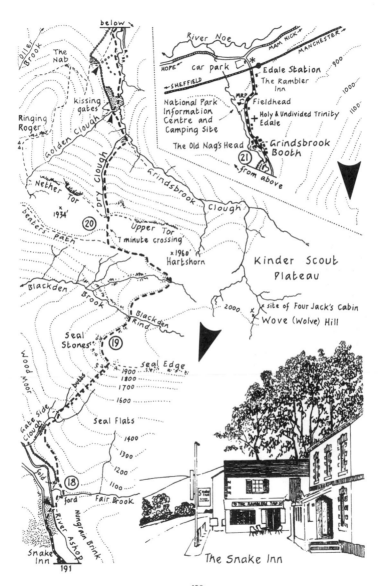

below

Oller Brook

The Nab

River Noe

MAM NICK

MANCHESTER

HOPE

car park

Edale Station

900

SHEFFIELD

The Rambler Inn

1000

kissing gates

MRP

Fieldhead

1100

Ringing Roger

National Park Information Centre and Camping Site

Holy & Undivided Trinity Edale

Golden Clough

The Old Nag's Head

Grindsbrook Booth

21

from above

Nether Tor

Dry Clough

Grindsbrook

x 1934'

20

Clough

beaters' PATH

Upper Tor

7 minute crossing

x 1960' Hartshorn

Kinder Scout Plateau

Blackden Brook

Blackden Rind

2000

site of Four Jack's Cabin

Wove (Wolve) Hill

Seal Stones

19

Seal Edge

1900
1800
1700
1600

Wood Moor

Gate Side Clough

butts

Seal Flats

1400

1300

1200

1100

18

fold

ford

Fair Brook

River Ashop

Nungain Brink

Snake Inn

191

THE RAMBLERS TAP

The Snake Inn

193

FURTHER READING

The Peak District: Roy Millward and Adrian Robinson (Eyre Methuen)

The Peak District: K.C.Edwards (Collins)

The Place-names of Derbyshire: Prof. Kenneth Cameron (Cambridge University Press)

The Royal Forest of the Peak: I.E.Burton (Peak Park J.P.B.)

Peakland Roads and Trackways: A.E. & E.M.Dodd (Moorland Publishing)

Freedom to Roam: Howard Hill (Moorland Publishing)

The 1932 Kinder Trespass: Benny Rothman (Willow Publishing)

High Peak Faces and Places: Keith Warrender (Pub. by author)

Moorland Heritage: James Byford (Pub. by author)

Peak and Pennines: W.A.Poucher (Constable)

A guide to the Pennine Way: C.J.Wright (Constable)

High Peak: E.Byne and G.J.Sutton (Secker and Warburg - out of print)

Across the Derbyshire Moors: John Derry (Loxley Bros. - out of print)

Rock Climbs in the Peak: various authors, a series of detailed guides produced for and by the Peak Committee of the B.M.C.

Safety on Mountains: John Jackson and B.M.C. (distributed by Cordee)

The Walkers' Handbook: H.D.Westacott (Penguin)

Mountaineering: Alan Blackshaw (Penguin)

First and Last: Roland Smith (Peak Park J.P.B.)

Moorland Erosion Study: (Peak Park J.P.B.)

Peak Park News: a quarterly journal reflecting current developments and environmental matters within the Park (Peak Park J.P.B)

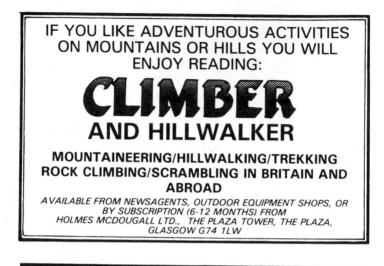